Explorations in Child Development
DVD Guide

for

Berk

Infants, Children, and Adolescents
Seventh Edition

prepared by

Amelia G. Benner

Sara Harris
Illinois State University

Laura E. Berk
Illinois State University

Allyn & Bacon

Boston   Columbus   Indianapolis   New York   San Francisco   Upper Saddle River
Amsterdam   Cape Town   Dubai   London   Madrid   Milan   Munich   Paris   Montreal   Toronto
Delhi   Mexico City   Sao Paulo   Sydney   Hong Kong   Seoul   Singapore   Taipei   Tokyo

10 9 8 7 6 5 4 3 2 V036 15 14 13 12 11

Allyn & Bacon
is an imprint of

www.pearsonhighered.com

ISBN-10: 0-205-01115-2
ISBN-13: 978-0-205-01115-5

CONTENTS

MIDDLE CHILDHOOD: SIX TO ELEVEN YEARS

ADOLESCENCE: THE TRANSITION TO ADULTHOOD

EMERGING ADULTHOOD

ACKNOWLEDGMENTS

I am indebted to many people for the opportunity to convey the beauty, wonderment, and complexity of child development through the new *Explorations in Child Development* DVD and accompanying Guide, designed to complement the seventh edition of *Infants, Children, and Adolescents*. This thoroughly revised DVD includes footage on wide-ranging topics, including 15 new segments addressing significant contemporary issues, such as pre-term birth, parenting a child with a genetic disorder, playful learning, autism, civic engagement in adolescence, and transition from college to adult life.

Phil Vandiver and Maria Henneberry of Contemporary Visuals in Bloomington, Illinois, were my collaborators as we filmed, wrote script, edited footage, and assembled the 47 segments into this DVD program. Maria and Phil's production talents, as well as their skill at recruiting and interviewing participants, were invaluable assets.

Many children, adolescents, parents, teachers, health professionals, and adults of all ages are responsible for the diversity of settings, concepts, and developmental milestones depicted in the DVD. Special thanks go to Karen Stephens, director of the Illinois State University Child Care Center in Normal, Illinois, who arranged for us to illustrate high-quality child care through interviews with children, parents, and teachers. Camille Taylor, guidance counselor at Normal Community High School, graciously helped us delve into students' experiences with peer harassment. Cindy Wulbert, Principal, facilitated several days of filming at Nettelhorst School in Chicago, enabling us to include several segments on high-quality elementary and middle-school education.

Finally, I want to express my appreciation to all the video participants, whose willingness to share their experiences yielded rich depictions of development and its diversity.

Laura E. Berk

INTRODUCTION

Explorations in Child Development **DVD** illustrates first-hand—through the everyday behaviors and responses of children, adolescents, and emerging adults—important theories, concepts, and milestones covered in Laura Berk's *Infants, Children, and Adolescents*, Seventh Edition. The DVD includes 47 segments on a wide range of topics, totaling several hours of fascinating and informative insights into the lives and minds of dozens of young people, as well as those who contribute vitally to their development.

The video segments have been designed for especially effective classroom use. They depict individuals personally affected by each topic, sometimes in extraordinary situations. Segment length ranges from 4 to 10 minutes, yielding a video experience ideally suited for in-class viewing and discussion.

The *Explorations in Child Development DVD Guide* helps students use the video segments to master course content, see the interconnectedness of all aspects of development, and apply their knowledge. After students view a video segment, corresponding questions in the guide can serve as a springboard for class discussion or an open-book assignment or quiz. Each question has been cross-referenced to relevant pages in the textbook.

Although many DVD segments are relevant to more than one text chapter, here are some suggestions:

Infants, Children, and Adolescents, **Seventh Edition**	**Suggested Video Segments**
Ch. 2: Genetic and Environmental Foundations	Down Syndrome Parenting a Child with a Genetic Disorder Rearing Multiples: Twins, and Triplets Reproductive Technology International Adoption
Ch. 4: Birth and the Newborn Baby	Childbirth Preterm Birth Transition to Parenthood Newborn Reflexes
Ch. 5: Physical Development in Infancy and Toddlerhood	Motor Development in Infancy
Ch. 6: Cognitive Development in Infancy and Toddlerhood	Language Development and Literacy
Ch. 7: Emotional and Social Development in Infancy and Toddlerhood	Early Emotional Development Custodial Grandparents Early Morally Relevant Self-Control

Ch. 9: Cognitive Development in Early Childhood	Piaget's Cognitive-Developmental Theory Piagetian Tasks Children's Understanding of Death Vygotsky's Sociocultural Theory Memory: Recognition, Recall, and Memory Strategies Autobiographical Memory Understanding of False Belief Autism Quality Child Care Jumpstart: Promoting Early Literacy and School Readiness Quality Child Care Playful Learning in Early Childhood
Ch. 10: Emotional and Social Development in Early Childhood	Moral Reasoning and Distributive Justice Child Abuse
Ch. 11: Physical Development in Middle Childhood	Childhood Obesity
Ch. 12: Cognitive Development in Middle Childhood	ADHD Cooperative Learning First-Grade Science Education Dramatic Arts Education Revitalizing an Inner-City School School–Community Partnership: After-School Enrichment Activities
Ch. 13: Emotional and Social Development in Middle Childhood	Self-Concept in Childhood and Adolescence Peer Harassment Custodial Grandparents Divorce and Father Custody
Ch. 14: Physical Development in Adolescence	Homosexuality Adolescent Parenthood
Ch. 16: Emotional and Social Development in Adolescence	Adolescent Friendship Adolescent Dating Civic Engagement in Adolescence Changing Parent–Child Relationships Delinquency
Ch. 17: Emerging Adulthood	Identity and Emerging Adulthood Resilience: From Gang Member to Responsible Adult Transition from College to Adult Life

Segment 1
Down Syndrome

Tonya and Steve faced a tragedy rare among couples in their twenties. Their first child, Kristin, was born with Down syndrome. Tonya and Steve describe their reaction to Kristin's birth and factors that helped them adjust to caring for a baby with serious developmental and health complications. They highlight the special role their younger daughter, Nicole, has played in Kristin's development.

For Discussion

1. In what ways are Kristin's physical features typical of Down syndrome? How about her health problems? (Chapter 2, p. 61)

   A. _____

   _____

   B. _____

   _____

2. Citing both the video and your text, explain why it is especially difficult to parent a baby with Down syndrome. (Chapter 2, p. 61)

   _____

   _____

   _____

   _____

3. What social and environmental factors have promoted Kristin's favorable development? How can Steve and Tonya help to improve Kristin's functioning in the future? (Chapter 2, p. 61)

   A. _____

   _____

   B. _____

   _____

4. Using the notion of canalization, explain why it was important to treat Kristin's health problems and provide her with an enriched environment at the earliest possible age. (Chapter 2, p. 84)

   _____

   _____

   _____

5. Because of her early experiences, Kristin does not crawl; she scoots. How will Kristin's motor development likely affect her interactions with the environment? (Chapter 5, p. 183)

   _____

   _____

Test Your Understanding

1. Most chromosomal defects result from errors during _____ (Chapter 2, p. 60)
   A. conception.
   B. pregnancy.
   C. mitosis.
   D. meiosis.

2. Statistically, Kristin's Down syndrome most likely resulted from _____ (Chapter 2, pp. 60–61)
   A. an extra twenty-first chromosome attached to part of another chromosome.
   B. oxygen deprivation before, during, or after birth.
   C. a failure of the twenty-first pair of chromosomes to separate during meiosis.
   D. prenatal malnutrition or exposure to environmental pollution.

3. Children with Down syndrome whose chromosomal abnormalities occur in a mosaic pattern are likely to display (less/more) extreme symptoms than those with other forms of Down syndrome. (Chapter 2, p. 61)

4. Steve and Tonya's situation is rare because _____ (Chapter 2, p. 61)
   A. younger parents are less likely to bear a baby with Down syndrome than older parents.
   B. children with Down syndrome are usually born to single mothers.
   C. Down syndrome is one of the least common chromosomal abnormalities.
   D. Down syndrome rarely results in slow motor development.

5. True or False: The father's gametes are sometimes responsible for the birth of a child with Down syndrome. (Chapter 2, p. 61)

Segment 2
Parenting a Child with a Genetic Disorder

Tiffany, age 13, is one of only a handful of children in the U.S. with Nijmegen Breakage Syndrome, a very rare genetic disorder that limits her growth and cognitive abilities and weakens her immune system. Tiffany's mother, Kathy, discusses the joys and challenges of parenting children with a severe illness—including the death of Tiffany's older sister Heather four years ago. Most children with the syndrome do not survive past their early teens, but Kathy says that she tries not to let Tiffany's condition limit her opportunities.

For Discussion

1. Kathy says that doctors were not aware that her daughters had Nijmegen Breakage Syndrome until after Tiffany was born. What types of prenatal tests are used to identify genetic disorders before birth? How might the Strehlows have benefited from genetic counseling? (Chapter 2, pp. 63–65)
    A. _____
    _____
    B. _____
    _____

2. Describe the early symptoms of Nijmegen Breakage Syndrome. Were the symptoms similar to those found in other genetic disorders? Explain. (Chapter 2, p. 60)
    A. _____
    _____
    B. _____
    _____

3. Tiffany participates in her school's special education program for children with cognitive impairments, which allows for both individualized attention and inclusive classes with other students. What are the benefits and limitations of inclusive classrooms for students with special needs? (Chapter 12, pp. 473–474)
    Benefits: _____
    _____
    Limitations: _____
    _____

4. How does Kathy's parenting style support Tiffany's independence and self-esteem? Provide examples from the video segment. (Chapter 13, p. 486)
    _____
    _____
    _____
    _____

Test Your Understanding

1. Nijmegen Breakage Syndrome _____ (Chapter 2, p. 60)
    A. is caused by exposure to teratogens.
    B. can be cured by gene therapy.
    C. is more common in females than in males.
    D. results from inheritance of two recessive alleles.

2. True or False: Genetic counseling is a process by which genetic disorders are treated prenatally. (Chapter 2, p. 63)

3. Teachers can foster peer acceptance of special-needs children by_____ (Chapter 12, p. 474)
    A. organizing group work and peer-tutoring experiences.
    B. pointing out students' differences and encouraging them to ask questions.
    C. creating lesson plans about developmental disabilities.
    D. providing extra supervision during nonacademic tasks.

4. True or False: Children with special needs benefit most when they are fully included in mainstream classrooms without separate instruction from special-education teachers. (Chapter 12, p. 473)

5. Kathy's warm, positive parenting style likely helps Tiffany by _____ (Chapter 13, p. 486)
    A. decreasing her hostility.
    B. increasing her competence.
    C. offsetting the symptoms of her disease.
    D. providing constant reassurance.

Segment 3
Rearing Multiples: Twins and Triplets

The Halbergs and the Bobells, two families living in the same neighborhood, are both familiar with the joys and challenges of multiple births. In this segment, the parents of the Halberg triplets and the Bobell twins discuss how their children forge their own identities within the family and how having multiples affects family life. Although both families say that sibling rivalries and limited time and resources can pose challenges, they also emphasize that raising multiples is a unique and rewarding experience.

For Discussion

1. Rates of multiple births have been increasing in North America for the past several decades. What factors have contributed to this increase? Which of these factors are mentioned in the video? (Chapter 2, p. 55)

   A. _____

   _____

   B. _____

   _____

2. Children of multiple births are often born earlier and develop more slowly than children of single births. How do the Halberg and Bobell children reflect this trend?
   (Chapter 2, pp. 55–56)

   _____

   _____

   _____

   _____

3. Studies indicate that parents of twins tend to focus on the distinctions between their children's personalities and talents rather on their children's similarities. How is this apparent in the Halbergs' and Bobells' assessments of their children's personalities? Do you, as an outside observer, consider the children quite different or very much alike?
   (Chapter 7, pp. 261–262)

   _____

   _____

   _____

4. Using examples from the video segment, explain how the Halberg and Bobell children establish their own unique roles within the family. (Chapter 13, pp. 508–509)

   _____

   _____

   _____

   _____

Test Your Understanding

1. The Halbergs say that fertility treatments led to the birth of their triplets. Other causes of multiple fraternal births include maternal age and _____ (Chapter 2, p. 55)
   A. family history of multiple births.
   B. mother's intake of folic acid.
   C. older paternal age.
   D. number of older siblings in the family.

2. True or False: Although children of multiple births often develop more slowly than children of single births, most catch up with their peers by middle childhood. (Chapter 2, pp. 55–56)

3. True or False: Due to hereditary factors, twins who are treated differently by their parents still develop similar temperaments. (Chapter 7, p. 261)

4. Among siblings who are the same age, _____ can spark sibling rivalries. (Chapter 13, p. 508)
   A. lack of guidance from older siblings
   B. time spent with grandparents
   C. parental comparison of siblings
   D. having the same close friends

5. To reduce rivalries and forge their own identities, many siblings, including multiples, _____ (Chapter 13, pp. 508–509)
   A. try to be as similar as possible.
   B. strive to excel in school and athletics.
   C. grow closer to their fathers than their mothers.
   D. purposefully adopt different interests and hobbies.

Segment 4

Reproductive Technology

Kim and Mike, in their thirties, discuss their experiences with infertility, including their efforts to become parents through various reproductive technologies. Kim describes her family history of infertility; both her mother and aunts had difficulty getting pregnant. After trying for years with several assisted reproductive techniques, Kim and Mike finally conceived. They discuss the stresses of infertility, the financial and emotional challenges of assisted reproduction, adjustment to pregnancy, and—after their twin sons are born—the transition to parenthood.

For Discussion

1. What were some of the challenges that Kim and Mike encountered while trying to conceive? How did they cope with these challenges?

   A. _____

   _____

   B. _____

   _____

2. In the video, the narrator describes a procedure called GIFT, which enabled Kim and Mike to conceive. What is GIFT, and how is it similar to in vitro fertilization? (Chapter 2, p. 66, Social Issues)

   A. _____

   _____

   B. _____

   _____

3. Kim and Mike express some of the fears they had when they discovered she was pregnant with twins. Using examples from the video and research presented in the text, list risk factors associated with multiple births. (Chapter 2, p. 67, Social Issues)

   _____

   _____

   _____

   _____

4. The text points out the importance of social support during pregnancy. Describe ways in which Mike supported Kim during her pregnancy. (Chapter 3, pp. 115, 116)

   _____

   _____

   _____

   _____

Test Your Understanding

1. Kim eventually gave birth to _____
   A. identical twins.
   B. fraternal twins.
   C. triplets.
   D. quadruplets.

2. _____ is/are a major cause of the dramatic rise in fraternal twinning and other multiple births in industrialized nations. (Chapter 2, p. 55)
   A. Younger maternal age
   B. Donor insemination
   C. In vitro fertilization
   D. Environmental teratogens

3. In the segment, Kim and Mike explain that they attempted in vitro fertilization four times. According to your text, the success rate of assisted reproductive techniques like in vitro fertilization is about ____ percent. (Chapter 2, p. 66, Social Issues)
   A. 15
   B. 25
   C. 35
   D. 65

4. How do Kim and Mike balance infant caregiving responsibilities?
   A. Kim primarily takes care of the twins and the household tasks.
   B. Mike primarily takes care of the twins and the household tasks.
   C. Kim and Mike both work part-time, dividing caregiving responsibilities so each is responsible for half.
   D. Kim and Mike share all aspects of caring for the twins.

5. Both the narrator and the text indicate that caregiving seems to be _____ for children conceived through donor insemination or in vitro fertilization. (Chapter 2, p. 67, Social Issues)
   A. warmer
   B. overly permissive
   C. less warm
   D. especially challenging

Segment 5
International Adoption

Jane Liedtke adopted her daughter, Emily, from a Chinese orphanage at the age of 17 months. Jane describes Emily's development from an underweight toddler with a limited vocabulary to the confident, intelligent adolescent that she has become. Emily's ethnic identity has thrived as a result of Jane's sensitive parenting and rich opportunities to immerse herself in the Chinese culture. Jane founded Our Chinese Daughters Foundation to help other adoptive parents embrace their children's Chinese heritage.

For Discussion

1. Cite several reasons why adopted children and adolescents may experience more learning and emotional difficulties than other children. (Chapter 2, p. 65)

   _____
   _____
   _____

2. What steps did Jane take to ensure that Emily developed a strong, secure ethnic identity? How is Emily likely to benefit from this positive identity development? (Chapter 16, p. 607, Cultural Influences)

   A. _____
   _____

   B. _____
   _____

3. If not for her adoption into a warm, supportive family, how might Emily's early experiences in an unstimulating orphanage have affected her development? (Chapter 4, pp. 169, 171)

   _____
   _____
   _____

4. Unlike many adoptees, Emily does not seem to struggle with unresolved curiosity about her roots. How do Jane and Emily explain this?

   _____
   _____
   _____

Test Your Understanding

1. True or False: International adoptees fare much better in development than birth siblings or institutionalized agemates who stay behind. (Chapter 2, p. 67)

2. Children placed in extremely deprived Romanian orphanages (Chapter 4, p. 171)
   A. show no lasting negative effects if adopted by age 2.
   B. rarely catch up with agemates' physical size, even after adoption.
   C. display appropriate reactions to stress, regardless of their time in the orphanage.
   D. for more than the first six months show serious intellectual deficits.

3. Emily became bilingual in childhood. As a result, she likely _____ (Chapter 12, p. 465)
   A. experienced cognitive and linguistic deficits.
   B. exhibits deficiencies in selective attention.
   C. experienced cognitive gains.
   D. is delayed in both her native language and English.

4. True or False: As a result of her exposure to Chinese history, traditions, values, language, and people, Emily is more likely to forge a favorable ethnic identity. (Chapter 16, p. 607, Cultural Influences)

5. Emily appears to have developed a(n) _____ identity—she has explored and adopted values from both the Chinese and American cultures. (Chapter 16, p. 607, Cultural Influences)

Name _____

Date _____

Segment 6
Childbirth

This segment follows Gina and her husband, Lindrey, through the labor and delivery of their second child. After the cesarean (surgical) delivery of her first child, Gina is determined to try a natural childbirth method this time. Supported by medical staff and her husband, Gina explores multiple positions and pain reduction techniques as she progresses through the stages of childbirth. Supported in an upright position, Gina successfully delivers a son, Christopher, without medical intervention.

For Discussion

1. Describe the infant's experience during labor, explaining how babies are equipped to handle the trauma of childbirth. (Chapter 4, p. 128)

   _____

   _____

   _____

2. Cite examples of social support during Gina's labor. How is this support likely to affect her birthing experience? (Chapter 4, pp. 130–131)

   A. _____

   _____

   B. _____

   _____

3. If Gina had used pain-relieving medication, how might her labor and delivery have been different? (Chapter 4, p. 133)

   _____

   _____

   _____

4. How can Gina and Lindry help their older child adapt to the arrival of a new sibling? (Chapter 7, pp. 276–277)

   _____

   _____

   _____

5. According to your text, how does a second birth typically affect the family system? How can Lindrey help Gina adjust to the arrival of Christopher? (Chapter 4, p. 156)

   A. _____

   _____

   B. _____

   _____

Test Your Understanding

1. Gina is eager to arrive at the _____ period of labor, when her cervix will open completely. (Chapter 4, p. 127, Figure 4.1)

2. When Gina's contractions become so close together that they are nearly constant, she is approaching stage _____. It won't be long before she feels the urge to push.
   (Chapter 4, p. 127)
   A. 1
   B. 2
   C. 3
   D. 4

3. Newborn Christopher received an Apgar score of 8. This means that he _____
   (Chapter 4, p. 128)
   A. is in good physical condition.
   B. requires special help in establishing vital signs.
   C. is in serious danger and requires emergency medical attention.
   D. has not taken a breath for 60 seconds.

4. True or False: Birth complications are common with home deliveries, even for healthy women who are assisted by a well-trained doctor or midwife. (Chapter 4, p. 132)

5. True or False: Older children often become more needy and demanding of their parents' attention when a new sibling arrives. (Chapter 7, p. 276)

Segment 7
Preterm Birth

Emma Bailey was stunned when she went into labor 22 weeks into her pregnancy. Bed rest helped delay the birth of her daughter Dani until 24 weeks, but the tiny baby still struggled to survive. Now a healthy toddler, Dani has not suffered any serious long-term effects of preterm birth, although her parents know that many other children not as lucky. In this segment, Emma and her husband Ed talk about the harrowing first months of Dani's life, including how the experience affected them.

For Discussion

1. Considering the information Emma provides in the video, cite factors that might have increased the risk of preterm birth.

   _____

   _____

   _____

2. Briefly describe the medical interventions that Dani received. How did medical staff attempt to recreate the conditions of the mother's uterus? (Chapter 4, pp. 138–139)

   A. _____

   _____

   B. _____

   _____

3. During her weeks in the hospital, why were stimulation and human contact with Dani so important? Use research from the text in your explanation. (Chapter 4, p. 138)

   _____

   _____

   _____

   _____

4. Explain how environmental advantages and warm parenting can help preterm infants catch up in development and avoid lasting problems. Use examples from the video. (Chapter 4, pp. 139–140)

   _____

   _____

   _____

   _____

Test Your Understanding

1. True or False: The risk of low birth weight rises with maternal age. (Chapter 3, p. 115)

2. _____ infants like Dani are born several weeks or more before their due date, while _____ infants are born on time, but below their expected weight. (Chapter 4, p. 137)
   A. Preterm; small-for-date
   B. Predate; underweight
   C. Small-for-date; preterm
   D. Antenatal; preterm

3. Preterm babies are cared for in small, enclosed beds called _____, to protect them from infection and control their body temperature. (Chapter 4, p. 138)
   A. kangaroo care centers
   B. incubators
   C. neonatal isolation units
   D. isolettes

4. True or False: Preterm babies rarely experience catch-up growth and typical development, even with a stable home environment and warm parental interaction. (Chapter 4, pp. 139–140)

5. In both developing and developed nations, _____ is an effective method of promoting survival and development of preterm infants. (Chapter 4, p. 138)
   A. isolation
   B. early intervention
   C. kangaroo care
   D. water therapy

Segment 8
Transition to Parenthood

Hilary and Derek, newlyweds in their thirties, discuss their first pregnancy and the arrival of their daughter, Lane. They explain how strong parenting role models and ties with extended family have helped them to prepare for parenthood. Hilary describes her recovery from a cesarean delivery and her initial struggles with breastfeeding. The importance of generous, paid maternity leave for both mothers and fathers is underscored. The couple's strong bond with each other and relaxed, flexible approach to everyday challenges have eased their transition, allowing them to enjoy their newborn.

For Discussion

1. How long a childbirth leave is necessary to ensure favorable maternal mental health and caregiving? Hilary's leave is considerably shorter. What risks are associated with childbirth leaves of six weeks or less? (Chapter 4, p. 140, Social Issues)

   A. _____

   B. _____

   _____

2. Summarize several ways in which Lane is likely to benefit from breastfeeding. (Chapter 5, p. 175, Applying What We Know)

   _____

   _____

   _____

3. How is Hilary and Derek's warm, considerate marriage likely to affect their parenting? (Chapter 2, p. 70)

   _____

   _____

   _____

4. List two factors that contribute to a couple's transition to parenthood. How are these factors likely to affect Hilary, Derek, and Lane? (Chapter 4, p. 154)

   A. _____

   _____

   B. _____

   _____

5. How are Hilary, Derek, and Lane likely to benefit from the social support of extended-family members who live nearby? (Chapter 2, p. 78)

   _____

   _____

   _____

Test Your Understanding

1. True or False: Because she became pregnant in her mid-thirties, Hilary faced a greater risk of prenatal and birth problems than mothers in their twenties. (Chapter 3, p. 115)

2. Which of the following is true about parental employment leave after childbirth in the United States? (Chapter 4, p. 140, Social Issues)
   A. Most new fathers take at least 10 weeks of employment leave.
   B. Most new mothers do not take the full 12 weeks of federally allotted maternity leave.
   C. The average length of maternity leave in the U.S. is sufficient to protect a new mother's well-being.
   D. Large U.S. companies are required to provide 12 weeks of paid maternity leave.

3. The narrator mentions that 2½ -week-old Lane is learning who her parents are. Research on infant–caregiver attachment indicates that Lane likely _____ (Chapter 7, p. 265)
   A. can recognize her mother's smell and voice.
   B. is strongly attached to her mother and father.
   C. will react with anger if left with an unfamiliar adult.
   D. prefers being held by her mother over her father.

4. Hilary enjoys her work and is also committed to parenting. As a result, Lane is likely to _____ as she grows up. (Chapter 13, p. 515)
   A. hold more gender-stereotyped beliefs
   B. experience authoritarian child rearing
   C. have lower self-esteem
   D. enjoy more positive family relations

5. True or False: The arrival of a baby causes significant marital strain for most new parents. (Chapter 4, p. 154)

Segment 9
Newborn Reflexes

This segment highlights a variety of newborn reflexes: rooting, sucking, eye blink, withdrawal, Babinski, Moro, palmar grasp, tonic neck, crawling, stepping, and escape. A demonstration of each reflex is accompanied by a brief discussion of its adaptive functions. Weak or absent reflexes, overly rigid or exaggerated reflexes, and reflexes that persist beyond the point when they should normally disappear can signal damage to the cerebral cortex.

For Discussion

1. Select two newborn reflexes, and describe how they form the basis for complex motor skills that will develop later. (Chapter 4, p. 144)

   A. _____

   _____

   B. _____

   _____

2. Select two newborn reflexes, and describe how they help parents and infants establish gratifying interaction. (Chapter 4, p. 144)

   A. _____

   _____

   B. _____

   _____

3. Why does the video illustrate reflexive capacities with babies no older than age 6 months? (Chapter 4, p. 145)

   _____

   _____

   _____

4. Describe the role of newborn reflexes in classical conditioning. (Chapter 5, p. 179)

   _____

   _____

   _____

5. Describe the role of newborn reflexes in the preattachment phase of Bowlby's ethological theory of attachment. (Chapter 7, p. 265)

   _____

   _____

   _____

Test Your Understanding

1. According to Bowlby's theory, the palmar grasp contributes to the development of attachment because it _____ (Chapter 7, p. 265)
   A. encourages social interaction between infants and caregivers.
   B. helps the baby cling to the mother during feeding.
   C. provides a foundation for later motor development.
   D. promotes emotional self-regulation.

2. Of the newborn reflexes that are not permanent, the _____ reflex typically disappears last. (Chapter 4, p. 144, Table 4.2)
   A. Babinski
   B. Moro
   C. rooting
   D. tonic neck

3. In human evolutionary past, the _____ reflex may have helped the infant cling to the mother. (Chapter 4, p. 144, Table 4.2)
   A. Babinski
   B. tonic neck
   C. Moro
   D. palmar grasp

4. True or False: Infants require special practice with the stepping reflex, or they will not walk at the typical age. (Chapter 4, p. 145)

5. Researchers believe that newborn reflexes disappear gradually as a result of development of the _____ (Chapter 4, p. 145)
   A. cerebellum.
   B. cerebral cortex.
   C. corpus callosum.
   D. hippocampus.

Name _____

Date _____

Segment 10
Motor Development in Infancy

This segment traces the attainment of a variety of gross- and fine-motor skills during the first two years, highlighting factors that influence these milestones, individual differences, and implications for other aspects of development. The union of perception and motor development is illustrated in children's responses to dropoffs.

For Discussion

1. Watch as 21-month-old Ben plays ball with Professor Berk and 18-month-old Katherine pushes a toy in playful circles around her mother. Describe several ways in which these motor developments are likely to influence parent-child interactions. (Chapter 5, p. 183)

   _____
   _____
   _____

2. Using the video, cite an example of motor development that generally follows the cephalocaudal trend and an example that follows the proximodistal trend. Then describe examples and evidence that deviate from these trends, along with implications of those deviations for our understanding of motor development. (Chapter 5, p. 162)
   Cephalocaudal: _____
   Proximodistal:_____
   Examples and evidence of deviations: _____
   _____
   Implications: _____
   _____

3. Using the example of 5-month-old Alex, who jumps with support from his father and struggles to crawl toward a rattle, explain why dynamic systems researchers argue that motor development cannot be a genetically prewired process. (Chapter 5, p. 185)

   _____
   _____
   _____

4. How are 8-month-old Randy's well-developed reaching abilities likely to affect his social interactions and exploration of the environment? (Chapter 5, pp. 187–188)

   _____
   _____
   _____

5. How do Alex, Hannah, Bailey, and Braxton's responses to a dropoff compare with research on the visual cliff? Why do their responses vary with crawling and walking experience? (Chapter 5, p. 192)

A. _____

_____

B. _____

_____

Test Your Understanding

1. True or False: If Kristin attends a preschool intervention program for children with disabilities, her motor skills are likely to show greater improvement than her intellectual performance. (Chapter 2, p. 61)

2. Why is the canalization of motor skills highly adaptive? (Chapter 2, p. 84)
   A. It ensures that children in a variety of environments will develop skills for survival.
   B. It promotes diversity, which is crucial for the evolution of more adaptive responses.
   C. It ensures that children with disadvantageous genes do not survive to reproduce.
   D. It encourages parents to rear their young in only the most advantageous environments.

3. Experience with the _____ reflex may eventually help Cara combine vision and arm movements into voluntary reaching. (Chapter 4, p. 144)
   A. rooting
   B. Moro
   C. tonic neck
   D. Babinski

4. Hannah's ability to crawl is an example of (fine-/gross-) motor development, while her capacity to grasp objects illustrates (fine-/gross-) motor development. (Chapter 4, p. 183)

5. True or False: Although motor development is a joint product of multiple factors, cultural attitudes and practices have little impact on the rate at which babies acquire motor skills. (Chapter 4, p. 186)

Name _____
Date _____

Segment 11
Language Development and Literacy

This segment highlights infant receptivity to language and characteristics of parent–infant interaction that help infants make sense of a complex speech stream. Several newborns and toddlers demonstrate early communicative capacities, first words, and the distinction between language comprehension and production. Zachary and Ben, who are nearing the end of their second year, highlight individual differences in early styles of language learning. Preschoolers and kindergartners playing and conversing display remarkable linguistic attainments in semantics, grammar, and pragmatics by the end of early childhood. Finally, Luke, Elena and Sophie's mothers read to them, illustrating rich parent–child dialogue.

For Discussion

1. Describe how Hannah's babbling is likely to evolve over the next several months. How might this progression differ if Hannah had been born deaf? (Chapter 6, p. 236)
   A. _____
   _____
   B. _____
   _____

2. One of Ben's first words is "ball." Why is this a typical word in children's early vocabularies? (Chapter 6, pp. 238–239)
   _____
   _____
   _____

3. How will her mother's use of child-directed speech likely affect 7-month-old Hannah's language development? (Chapter 6, p. 242)
   _____
   _____
   _____

4. Cite evidence that Luke, Sophie, and Elena are engaged in interactive reading. How are such experiences likely to benefit the children's development? (Chapter 9, p. 343)
   A. _____
   _____
   B. _____
   _____

Test Your Understanding

1. If Luke is like most 18-month-olds, he _____ (Chapter 6, p. 237, Table 6.3)
    A. has not said his first word yet.
    B. produces more words than he comprehends.
    C. communicates primarily by cooing.
    D. will soon produce two-word utterances.

2. Sophie and Elena's mother engages them in _____ attention, in which she attends to the same book as her daughters. (Chapter 6, p. 238)

3. True or False: At all ages, children understand more words than they regularly use. (Chapter 6, p. 240)

4. True or False: Piaget regarded language as the primary ingredient in childhood cognitive change. (Chapter 9, p. 318)

5. Luke "reads" by naming pictures in storybooks with his mother. This is an example of _____ (Chapter 9, p. 343)
    A. child-directed speech.
    B. emergent literacy.
    C. phonological awareness.
    D. fast-mapping.

Name _____

Date _____

Segment 12
Early Emotional Development

This segment underscores the role of emotions in organizing and regulating many aspects of experience. Emotional milestones of infancy—the social smile, laughter, fear (including stranger anxiety), use of the caregiver as a secure base, and social referencing—are illustrated. The children also demonstrate various aspects of temperament, including sociability, attention span, activity level, and persistence. Next, the video depicts milestones of attachment, such as newborn capacities that evoke loving care, emotional responsiveness to the familiar caregiver, appearance of clear-cut attachment (including separation anxiety), and the capacity to tolerate short parental absences. Finally, emergence of self-recognition is explored by dabbing red dye on toddlers' noses and watching how they react to their changed appearance in a mirror.

For Discussion

1. Cite factors that influence infants' stranger anxiety. How can caregivers and unfamiliar adults reduce this fear? (Chapter 7, p. 252)

    A. _____

    _____

    B. _____

    _____

2. How is social referencing likely to expand Randy's understanding of emotions? (Chapter 7, p. 253)

    _____

    _____

    _____

3. Katherine appears sociable in this segment, while Ben seems shy. Cite several ways in which their physiological responses to novel stimuli are likely to differ. (Chapter 7, p. 259, Biology and Environment)

    _____

    _____

    _____

    _____

4. How do children benefit from play with fathers? Explain, citing research presented in the text. (Chapter 7, p. 276, Cultural Influences)

    _____

    _____

    _____

5. Describe experiences that promote the development of self-awareness and self-recognition. (Chapter 7, pp. 280–281)

_____

_____

_____

Test Your Understanding

1. Randy's expression of sadness illustrates a (basic/self-conscious) emotion, while Zachary's embarrassed reaction to the red dye on his nose exemplifies a (basic/self-conscious) emotion. (Chapter 7, pp. 250, 253–254)

2. Newborn Anna Marie does not mind being left with an unfamiliar adult like Professor Berk. She grasps Professor Berk to maintain closeness. According to Bowlby's ethological theory of attachment, Anna Marie is in the _____ phase of attachment. (Chapter 7, p. 265)
   A. preattachment
   B. "attachment in the making"
   C. "clear-cut" attachment
   D. formation of a reciprocal relationship

3. True or False: All children experience separation anxiety. (Chapter 7, p. 265)

4. Hannah appears upset when her mother leaves the room. When her mother returned off-camera, she was comforted easily. Hannah has likely developed a(n) _____ attachment to her mother. (Chapter 7, pp. 266–267)
   A. avoidant
   B. secure
   C. resistant
   D. disorganized

5. True or False: Bowlby believed that attachment is an evolved response that promotes survival by forging a bond between the infant and caretaker. (Chapter 7, p. 265)

Segment 13
Custodial Grandparents

In this segment, Marcella Davenport shares her experiences raising 4-year-old Dominic, her great-grandson. Marcella and her husband assumed custody of Dominic from their troubled granddaughter. Marcella explains that she and her husband wanted to provide a stable, protective home and good life for their great-grandson. They had serious concerns at first, but now say that Dominic has greatly enriched their lives.

For Discussion

1. When they first considered raising Dominic, what concerns did the Davenports have? Why did they ultimately decide to adopt him?

   A. _____

   _____

   _____

   B. _____

   _____

   _____

2. According to the text, what difficulties do adopted children often face? What factors contribute to these difficulties? Why might children like Dominic, being reared by grandparents because of their birth mother's inability to care for them, be at risk for similar problems? (Chapter 2, pp. 65–66)

   A. _____

   _____

   B. _____

   _____

   C. _____

   _____

   _____

3. Marcella mentions that she recently enrolled Dominic in child care. Until that point, he had spent most of his time with adults and had little experience interacting with peers. How has Dominic adjusted to being in child care? According to the text, what characteristics of the child-care environment will help Dominic develop favorably? (Chapter 9, p. 351)

   A. _____

   _____

   B. _____

   _____

   _____

4. Marcella describes the challenges of raising a young child later in life. What concerns does she have about being older than other parents?

_____

_____

_____

_____

Test Your Understanding

1. Adopted children and adolescents _____ than other children. (Chapter 2, p. 65)
   A. have fewer learning and emotional difficulties
   B. have more learning and emotional difficulties
   C. are more likely to receive authoritative child rearing
   D. are happier and more grateful to their parents

2. True or False: The number of grandparents raising grandchildren has increased over the past two decades. (Chapter 7, p. 275)

3. True or False: Children being reared by custodial grandparents show high rates of learning difficulties. (Chapter 7, p. 275)

4. Warm child-grandparent relationships can often shield children from _____ (Chapter 7, pp. 275–276)
   A. worsening adjustment problems.
   B. developing healthy relationships with their parents.
   C. growing up in poverty.
   D. substance abuse.

5. Looking back at her decision to adopt Dominic, Marcella _____
   A. regrets taking full custody.
   B. feels that she was manipulated into taking him.
   C. hopes that she can be a role model to other grandparents who are raising grandchildren.
   D. focuses on the positive aspects of being a mother.

Segment 14
Early Morally Relevant Self-Control

In this segment, 1½–year-old Luke and 2½-year-old twins Sophie and Elena demonstrate their ability to comply with adult directives as they retrieve various objects. Next, Professor Berk presents a delay-of-gratification task to 2-year-old Peter and to Sophie and Elena. Notice how Peter immediately eats the M&Ms, whereas Sophie and Elena wait for Professor Berk to return before eating the candy. In a second delay-of-gratification task, Sophie and Elena again demonstrate self-control as they wait for Professor Berk to return before looking in a bag for presents.

For Discussion

1. What two cognitive capacities enable 20-month-old Luke to behave in a self-controlled fashion? (Chapter 7, p. 282)
   A. _____
   _____
   B. _____
   _____

2. Describe parenting techniques that foster children's capacity for delay of gratification. (Chapter 7, p. 283)
   _____
   _____
   _____

3. Although Peter is nearly the same age as Sophie and Elena, he exhibits poorer performance on the delay-of-gratification task. Summarize factors that may have contributed to this difference. (Chapter 7, p. 283)
   _____
   _____
   _____

4. How would Vygotsky's sociocultural theory likely explain the relationship between the acceleration in vocabulary growth and increases in self-control during the second year? (Chapter 9, pp. 329–330)
   _____
   _____
   _____

5. What self-control strategies do Sophie and Elena use during the delay-of-gratification tasks?
   _____
   _____
   _____

Test Your Understanding

1. True or False: For most toddlers, opposition is far more common than compliance.
   (Chapter 7, p. 282)

2. (Girls/Boys) are typically more self-controlled. (Chapter 7, p. 283)

3. True or False: Toddlers' control over their own actions requires little parental oversight.
   (Chapter 7, p. 283)

4. Peter's mother can help her son develop compliance and self-control by _____
   (Chapter 7, p. 283, Applying What We Know)
   A. ignoring Peter's self-controlled behavior.
   B. offering many prompts and reminders.
   C. gradually decreasing the number of rules Peter is expected to follow.
   D. forcing Peter to comply with her requests.

5. While waiting to open the presents, Sophie says, "Lie down for wait to her." Her mother
   responds, "OK, you're going to lie down to wait for her." This is an example of
   _____ (Chapter 9, p. 359)
   A. recasting.
   B. overregularization.
   C. fast-mapping.
   D. the mutual exclusivity bias.

Segment 15
Piaget's Cognitive-Developmental Theory

After a brief review of Piaget's stages and his view of the child as an active seeker of knowledge, major Piagetian milestones are illustrated. These include development of object permanence in infancy; rapid changes in representation during the second year (including emergence of categorization and make-believe play); gains in ability to conserve, seriate, and categorize flexibly from early to middle childhood; and emergence of hypothetico-deductive reasoning and propositional thought in adolescence.

For Discussion

1. How might 8-month-old Randy's performance on the object-finding task differ if his mother deposited the toy under the cloth with her hand, rather than covering the toy with the cloth? (Chapter 6, p. 207)

   _____

   _____

   _____

2. Watch as 4-year-old Alison engages in make-believe play about train crashes with her father and brother. Cite evidence of the preschool child's growing symbolic mastery in this segment. (Chapter 9, p. 319)

   _____

   _____

   _____

3. How is Alison likely to benefit from her rich experiences with sociodramatic play? (Chapter 9, pp. 319–320)

   _____

   _____

   _____

4. Using an example from the video and research presented in the text, explain how problem solving at the formal operational stage differs from problem solving in the concrete operational stage. (Chapter 15, pp. 566–567)

   _____

   _____

   _____

5. What aspects of moral development are evident in the high school students' discussion of Martin Luther? How does peer interaction, such as that depicted in the video, promote moral understanding? (Chapter 16, pp. 609–611, 614)

   A. _____

   _____

   B. _____

   _____

Test Your Understanding

1. True or False: Piaget regarded goal-directed action sequences, such as finding a hidden toy, as the foundation for all problem solving. (Chapter 6, p. 207)

2. Ben, who is 21 months old, engages in make-believe play with a toy telephone. This is made possible by his capacity for _____ and indicates that he is in Piaget's sensorimotor Substage _____. (Chapter 6, p. 205)
   A. circular reactions; 1
   B. object permanence; 3
   C. the A-not-B search error ; 5
   D. mental representation; 6

3. When attempting the conservation-of-liquid task, Stephen explains his incorrect answer by stating that the dish is bigger than the glass. Stephen _____ the size of the dish. (Chapter 9, p. 322)
   A. represents
   B. conserves
   C. centers on
   D. reverses

4. Follow-up research indicates that 18-month-old Katherine and 4-year-old Zach, who categorize shapes by color in the video, probably (are/are not) capable of classification on the basis of nonobvious properties. (Chapter 9, p. 326)

5. A student in the high school math class justifies his reasoning by _____, which suggests that logical thought _____. (Chapter 15, pp. 567–568)
   A. giving a concrete example; appears suddenly around the time of puberty
   B. giving a concrete example; develops gradually
   C. explaining logical rules; appears suddenly around the time of puberty
   D. explaining logical rules; develops gradually

Name _____

Date _____

Segment 16
Piagetian Tasks

This segment depicts children's performance on a variety of Piagetian tasks. Four-year-olds Alison and Stephen have difficulty with conservation of liquid, number, and length. However, when conservation-of-number and mass tasks are simplified and made relevant to her everyday experience, Alison demonstrates accurate, logical reasoning. Five-year-old Nicole struggles with a class inclusion task, while 7-year-olds Victor and Zoe succeed. Participants explain their reasoning, illustrating important features of Piaget's preoperational and concrete operational stages.

For Discussion

1. Cite examples of centration and irreversibility in Alison and Stephen's reasoning. (Chapter 9, p. 322)

    _____

    _____

    _____

2. According to follow-up research on preoperational thought, why did Alison's performance on the conservation of number task improve when she was presented with only three chips? (Chapter 9, p. 324)

    _____

    _____

    _____

3. Describe experiences and developments that support preschoolers' skills at categorizing. (Chapter 9, pp. 324–325)

    _____

    _____

    _____

4. In what order did Victor and Zoe likely master Piaget's conservation tasks? What does this reveal about concrete operational thinking? (Chapter 12, p. 440)

    A. _____

    B. _____

5. Describe cultural experiences that may have contributed to Zoe and Victor's mastery of Piagetian tasks. (Chapter 12, pp. 440–441)

    _____

    _____

    _____

Test Your Understanding

1. Nicole has difficulty with the hierarchical classification task, indicating that her thought is characterized by _____ (Chapter 9, p. 322)
   A. animistic thinking.
   B. centration.
   C. conservation.
   D. reversibility.

2. Alison's performance on the simplified conservation of number task (supports/refutes) Piaget's assertion that preschoolers are incapable of operations. (Chapter 9, p. 324)

3. Alison and Stephen are likely to develop a deeper understanding of gender constancy as their capacity for _____ improves. (Chapter 10, p. 396)
   A. centration
   B. spatial reasoning
   C. seriation
   D. conservation

4. Zoe and Victor are in Piaget's concrete operational stage. They are likely to perform poorly on _____ tasks. (Chapter 12, p. 440)
   A. hypothetical transitive inference
   B. conservation
   C. hierarchical classification
   D. seriation

5. True or False: Performance on Piagetian tasks develops uniformly across cultures. (Chapter 12, p. 440)

Segment 17
Children's Understanding of Death

This segment opens with 4-year-olds Lucy and Drake responding to questions that assess their understanding of death. While Lucy clearly distinguishes between animate and inanimate objects, she lacks a complete grasp of the irreversibility of death. Drake's developing understanding of the death concept is revealed as he reflects on the deaths of his grandparents. Next, interviews with 8-year-old Chandler and 11-year-old Izzy illustrate significant gains in death understanding over middle childhood. Chandler's religious background influences some of his beliefs about death. Izzy's greater biological knowledge enables her to provide thoughtful, detailed explanations.

For Discussion

1. An accurate understanding of death is based on five ideas:
    Permanence (Death is irreversible.)
    Inevitability (All living things eventually die.)
    Cessation (All living functions cease at death.)
    Applicability (Death only applies to living things.)
    Causation (Death is caused by a disruption in bodily functioning.)
    Which concepts do Lucy and Drake clearly understand? Which concepts are challenging for them? Explain, citing examples from the video.
    Clear understanding: _____
    _____
    _____
    Challenging concepts: _____
    _____
    _____

2. How does Lucy display magical thinking in her explanations about death? (Chapter 9, pp. 323–324)
    _____
    _____

3. How do Chandler's beliefs about the afterlife reflect his understanding of God? (Chapter 13, p. 495, Cultural Influences)
    _____
    _____

4. Using examples from the video, explain how children's biological knowledge affects their grasp of the death concept. (Chapter 13, p. 495, Cultural Influences)
    _____
    _____
    _____

Test Your Understanding

1. True or False: Piaget claimed that young children frequently attribute psychological characteristics, such as the ability to feel and think, to inanimate objects. (Chapter 9, p. 321)

2. Lucy is more likely to use magical explanations for phenomena she has not personally experienced than for those that are familiar. For instance, she understands that death is irreversible for humans, but she believes that magic tricks might bring a grasshopper back to life. This (supports/refutes) Piaget's view of the limitations of preoperational thought. (Chapter 9, pp. 323–324)

3. Young children like Chandler frequently envision God as a formless, omnipotent, and abstract force. (Chapter 13, p. 495, Cultural Influences)

4. Drake's understanding of the death concept is limited because he
   A. has never experienced the death of a friend or relative.
   B. believes that sleep and death are interchangeable.
   C. has not mastered most Piagetian tasks.
   D. cannot distinguish between animate beings and inanimate objects.

5. True or False: Young children often explain death in terms of familiar experiences, citing changes in behavior, such as "you can't talk or walk."

Segment 18
Vygotsky's Sociocultural Theory

This segment depicts Vygotsky's emphasis on social dialogues as a major source of cognitive development. First-grade students demonstrate private speech as they work through a math assignment. Four-year-old Emily solves a challenging shape puzzle with appropriate scaffolding from her mother. Sophie, age 2½, collaborates with her father in rich, imaginative make-believe play. Finally, fourth-grade students employ cooperative learning as they solve a math problem.

For Discussion

1. How is Sophie likely to benefit from engaging in joint make-believe with her father? (Chapter 6, p. 226, Cultural Influences)

   _____

   _____

   _____

2. The first-grade students speak aloud to themselves as they work on a challenging math problem. How does Piaget explain the function of such speech? How does Vygotsky's explanation differ? (Chapter 9, p. 330)

   Piaget: _____

   _____

   Vygotsky: _____

   _____

3. How is the first-grade students' private speech likely to change with age? (Chapter 9, p. 330)

   _____

   _____

   _____

4. How is Emily likely to benefit from her mother's effective scaffolding? (Chapter 9, p. 331)

   _____

   _____

   _____

5. What benefits are associated with cooperative learning? (Chapter 12, p. 470)

   _____

   _____

   _____

Test Your Understanding

1. (Piaget/Vygotsky) would assert that Sophie discovered make-believe independently, while (Piaget/Vygotsky) would attribute the advancement of Sophie's make-believe capacities to her father's guidance. (Chapter 6, p. 226, Cultural Influences)

2. A child is least likely to use private speech if he _____ (Chapter 9, p. 330)
   A. is appropriately challenged.
   B. has recently made an error.
   C. is confused about how to proceed.
   D. faces a very difficult task.

3. Emily and her mother collaborate on a shape-fitting puzzle. This task is within Emily's _____; it is too difficult for her to complete alone but possible with her mother's help. (Chapter 9, p. 330)

4. Which of the following is true of most Vygotskyian classrooms? (Chapter 9, p. 332)
   A. Independent discovery is often their sole focus.
   B. They promote assisted discovery through collaboration.
   C. They downplay the significance of make-believe.
   D. Peer collaboration is discouraged, as it promotes inaccurate reasoning.

5. True or False: Cooperative learning requires extensive training and guidance in order to succeed. (Chapter 12, p. 470)

Segment 19

Memory: Recognition, Recall, and Memory Strategies

As 4-year-old Stephen and 7-year-old Victor play a memory game, they demonstrate that recognition develops ahead of recall. Victor's comments illustrate the development of memory strategies and metacognition in middle childhood. Seven-year-old Zoe further demonstrates metacognitive awareness as she describes her use of categorization as a memory aid.

For Discussion

1. Why did Stephen find the recognition task easier than the recall task? (Chapter 9, p. 336)

   _____

   _____

   _____

2. Why do young children seldom use memory strategies? (Chapter 9, p. 336)

   _____

   _____

   _____

3. How have cultural circumstances likely affected the development of Victor and Zoe's memory strategies? (Chapter 12, p. 440)

   _____

   _____

   _____

4. Summarize differences in metacognitive awareness between 4-year-old Stephen and 7-year-old Victor that contribute to their differing capacities for recall. (Chapter 9, pp. 338–339; Chapter 12, pp. 447–449)

   Stephen: _____

   _____

   Victor: _____

   _____

Test Your Understanding

1. In which part of the information-processing system does Zoe actively apply mental strategies, such as categorization? (Chapter 6, pp. 217–218)
   A. sensory register
   B. working memory
   C. long-term memory
   D. memory span

2. (Recall/Recognition) involves determining whether a stimulus is the same as or similar to previous stimuli. (Recall/Recognition) requires a person to generate a mental image of an absent stimulus. (Chapter 9, p. 336)

3. True or False: Given a challenging list of items to learn, 4-year-old Stephen is likely to engage in the memory strategies of rehearsal and organization. (Chapter 9, p. 336)

4. Based on his age, which of the following is likely true of 4-year-old Stephen's metacognitive awareness? Stephen _____ (Chapter 9, p. 341)
   A. overestimates the amount of mental activity that goes on in people.
   B. can infer what people know or are thinking about.
   C. views the mind as a passive container of information.
   D. engages in planning and uses memory strategies often.

5. True or False: By middle childhood, children are able to use several memory strategies at once. (Chapter 12, p. 446)

Segment 20
Autobiographical Memory

Using an elaborative communication style, Stephen and Alison's parents elicit their children's narratives about a recent trip to the zoo. They ask numerous, varied questions; provide information to aid recall; and volunteer some of their own recollections and evaluations. As a result, Stephen and Alison are able to discuss this autobiographical memory in great detail.

For Discussion

1. Explain why infantile amnesia cannot be attributed merely to the passage of time. (Chapter 6, p. 221, Biology and Environment)

   _____
   _____
   _____

2. Review Vygotsky's concept of the zone of proximal development. Then, using examples from the video, explain how the elaborative style of communication creates a zone of proximal development for Stephen and Alison. (Chapter 6, p. 224; Chapter 9, p. 337)

   _____
   _____
   _____

3. Imagine that Larry and Linda used a repetitive communication style instead of an elaborative style. How might this have altered Stephen and Alison's responses? (Chapter 9, p. 337)

   _____
   _____
   _____

4. Discuss the effects of parent–child reminiscence on children's self-understanding. (Chapter 9, p. 337)

   _____
   _____
   _____

Test Your Understanding

1. If Stephen and Alison visited the zoo often, perhaps a couple of times per week, they might form a(n) _____ to help them organize and interpret these visits. (Chapter 9, p. 337)

2. Because Linda and Larry use the elaborative style when reminiscing with their children, we can infer they are most likely (insecurely/securely) attached to their children. (Chapter 9, p. 337)

3. Alison provides a more elaborate account of the trip to the zoo than Stephen does. How might memory researchers explain this difference? (Chapter 9, p. 337)
   A. Stephen's memory utilizes a repetitive style of information processing.
   B. Parents reminisce in greater detail with daughters than with sons.
   C. Stephen has not yet developed a script for visiting the zoo.
   D. Stephen is experiencing infantile amnesia.

4. Alison responds to her father's question about snakes, adding, "Would you want to have one of those for your pet?" She demonstrates advances in the practical, social side of language, known as _____ (Chapter 9, p. 358)
   A. grammar.
   B. semantic bootstrapping.
   C. overregularization.
   D. pragmatics.

5. True or False: Preschoolers rarely use memory strategies because space in their working memories is limited. (Chapter 9, p. 336)

Segment 21
Understanding of False Belief

During the preschool years, children begin to form a theory of mind—a coherent understanding of mental life—although their grasp of some concepts develops gradually. Four-year-old Logan does not yet understand false belief, while 7-year-old Zoe's ability to predict where a puppet will look for Band-Aids reveals clear understanding. Zoe also demonstrates cognitive gains in middle childhood as she successfully solves a second-order false-belief task.

For Discussion

1. How will Logan likely benefit from further development of belief-desire reasoning?
   (Chapter 9, p. 339)

   _____
   _____
   _____

2. Cite several factors that contribute to children's mastery of false-belief tasks.
   (Chapter 9, pp. 339–340)

   _____
   _____
   _____

3. What does Zoe's sophisticated response to the false-belief tasks indicate about her theory of mind? (Chapter 12, p. 448)

   _____
   _____
   _____

4. How is Zoe's appreciation of second-order false belief likely to affect her social skills?
   (Chapter 12, p. 448)

   _____
   _____
   _____

5. How do Logan's and Zoe's responses compare with Selman's stages of perspective taking?
   (Chapter 13, pp. 491–492)

   _____
   _____
   _____

Test Your Understanding

1. Piaget would probably explain Logan's performance on the false-belief task by stating that Logan is _____ (Chapter 9, p. 339)
   A. in the formal operational stage.
   B. exhibiting egocentric thinking.
   C. not yet capable of conservation.
   D. engaging in animistic thinking.

2. True or False: Logan is probably aware that thinking takes place inside her head. (Chapter 9, p. 339)

3. Logan has not yet mastered the false-belief task. This indicates that she probably thinks people's behavior is influenced by _____. (Chapter 9, p. 339)
   A. beliefs
   B. desires
   C. beliefs and desires
   D. false beliefs

4. True or False: Children's theory of mind develops uniformly across cultures, regardless of schooling. (Chapter 12, p. 448)

5. Children like Zoe, who have an understanding of second-order false belief, are able to _____ (Chapter 12, p. 448)
   A. pinpoint the reasons that another person arrived at a certain belief.
   B. engage in hypothetico-deductive reasoning.
   C. effectively coordinate moral, social-conventional, and personal concerns.
   D. engage in divergent thinking.

Segment 22
Autism

Brad and Becky have two sons who show symptoms of autism spectrum disorder. Matthew, the elder, has Asperger syndrome, a milder form, while Andrew, the younger, has autism. Their parents describe the progression of Andrew's condition, as well as the day-to-day and long-term challenges they face as they search for ways to help their children.

For Discussion

1. Using research in the text and examples from the video, what symptoms of autism does Andrew display? (Chapter 9, p. 342, Biology and Environment)

   _____

   _____

   _____

2. Explain how Brad and Becky discovered that Andrew has autism.

   _____

   _____

   _____

   _____

3. Using examples from the video, what child-rearing style does Brad and Becky use with their sons? Given the boys' challenges, does their approach seem effective? Explain. (Chapter 10, pp. 398–400)

   A. _____

   _____

   B. _____

   _____

4. What kinds of social support does the family have? How might Brad and Becky benefit from these relationships as they face the challenges of raising children with autism? (Chapter 11, p. 424)

   Support: _____

   _____

   Benefits: _____

   _____

Test Your Understanding

1. Researchers agree that autism is caused by _____, usually due to
    _____. (Chapter 9, p. 342, Biology and Environment)
    A. abnormal brain functioning; genetic or prenatal environmental causes
    B. poor maternal nutrition during pregnancy; poverty or child neglect
    C. oxygen deprivation at birth; medical mistakes
    D. impaired nervous system functioning; prenatal exposure to lead

2. Researchers believe the deviant growth pattern of the _____ leads to deficits in
    emotion processing and social interaction in children with autism. (Chapter 9, p. 342,
    Biology and Environment)
    A. cerebellum
    B. amygdala
    C. corpus callosum
    D. central nervous system

3. True or False: Despite other cognitive deficiencies, children with autism are often skilled at
    understanding false belief and at attributing mental states to others. (Chapter 9, p. 342,
    Biology and Environment)

4. True or False: Children with autism engage in less make-believe play than other children.
    (Chapter 9, p. 342, Biology and Environment)

5. Early symptoms of autism that parents often notice in their children are _____.
    (Chapter 9, p. 342, Biology and Environment)
    A. high-pitched crying and irregular sleep patterns
    B. frequent ear infections and impaired gross-motor skills
    C. precocious use of language and lack of stranger anxiety
    D. delays in language learning and lack of social interaction

Name _____
Date _____

Segment 23
Quality Child Care

The Illinois State University Child Care Center in Normal, Illinois, offers high-quality, low-cost child care to university students, staff, and faculty. Vera, a single mother and full-time student, describes how the center nurtures her daughter, Empress, both intellectually and emotionally. Barb, one of Empress's teachers, elaborates on how caregiving at the center strives to foster lasting socioemotional skills, while director Karen explains the center's guiding philosophies and highlights the role of social policy in U.S. child care.

For Discussion

1. Instructors at the Center guide Empress in labeling and discussing her emotions. Her mother continues this practice at home. How is Empress likely to benefit from such dialogues? (Chapter 10, p. 368)

    _____
    _____
    _____

2. Cite several benefits associated with high-quality, center-based child care during the preschool years. (Chapter 9, p. 349)

    _____
    _____
    _____

3. Karen mentions that poor-quality child care can be detrimental to children's development. Cite developmental outcomes associated with high- and low-quality child care. (Chapter 9, p. 351)
    High-quality child care: _____

    _____
    Low-quality child care: _____

    _____

4. Identify several signs of developmentally appropriate early childhood programs at the ISU Child Care Center. (Chapter 9, p. 352)

    _____
    _____
    _____

5. Are Empress's ideas about friendship typical for her age? Explain, citing examples from your text and from the video. (Chapter 10, pp. 374–375)

    _____
    _____
    _____

Test Your Understanding

1. True or False: Children who spend long hours in poor-quality child care often display behavioral problems and score lower in cognitive skills. (Chapter 9, p. 351)

2. Because Empress does not have any siblings, she is less likely to _____ in school than children with siblings. (Chapter 13, p. 508)
    A. exhibit high self-esteem
    B. have close, high-quality friendships
    C. earn high grades
    D. be accepted in her peer group

3. The caregiver–child ratio at the Child Care Center is one adult to every five children. This (does not meet/matches/exceeds) developmentally appropriate standards for early childhood programs. (Chapter 9, p. 352, Applying What We Know)

4. Empress says that she is "everybody's friend." With age, she will most likely _____ (Chapter 13, p. 499)
    A. become less selective about her friendships.
    B. become more selective about her friendships.
    C. maintain her current number of friendships.
    D. experience a decline in friendship stability.

5. At the Child Care Center, students and teachers often collaborate on projects tailored to students' interests. Symbolic communication, such as writing, is emphasized. Which of the following theories might have influenced the Center's practices? (Chapter 12, p. 468)
    A. Montessori
    B. Piaget
    C. traditional
    D. Vygotsky

Segment 24
Jumpstart: Promoting Early Literacy and School Readiness

Jumpstart is a nonprofit organization that trains college and university students (called Corps members) to provide preschoolers from low-income families with intensive early literacy and other school-readiness intervention, increasing the changes that they will succeed academically after school entry. Parents, teachers, and volunteers emphasize that Jumpstart helps create a strong foundation on which students can build an education.

For Discussion

1. Consider research in Chapter 2 of your text about the impact of environment, family, and socioeconomic status on development. How do programs like Jumpstart work to overcome negative environmental circumstances? (Chapter 2, pp. 71–75)

   _____
   _____
   _____
   _____

2. How does Jumpstart help preschoolers develop literacy skills? Be sure to consider research on how young children learn to process written language. (Chapter 9, pp. 343–344)

   _____
   _____
   _____
   _____

3. In Chapter 9, you learned about the differences between child-centered and academic education programs for young children. Which approach does Jumpstart follow, or does it combine aspects of both? Explain. (Chapter 9, p. 348)

   _____
   _____
   _____
   _____

4. Jumpstart stresses the importance of early intervention for children who are at-risk for poor school readiness. How do programs like Jumpstart contribute to children's long-term performance in school? (Chapter 9, pp. 349–350)

   _____
   _____
   _____
   _____

Test Your Understanding

1. True or False: Parents in lower-SES households usually provide their children with similar amounts of verbal stimulation and at-home education as those in higher-SES households. (Chapter 2, p. 72)

2. Preschoolers develop written language skills more quickly when adults _____ (Chapter 9, p. 345)
   A. let children look at books on their own.
   B. give children lists of words to memorize.
   C. discuss the content of books and sound out words while reading aloud.
   D. stress the importance of reciting the alphabet.

3. Research indicates that children who _____ tend to perform better in school and develop literacy skills than the average. (Chapter 9, p. 345)
   A. have imaginary friends
   B. begin to speak at a younger age
   C. attend child care
   D. live in homes filled with books and educational toys

4. Early-intervention programs like Jumpstart are most effective when _____ (Chapter 9, p. 350)
   A. parents are involved in their child's education and extend lessons from the program into the home.
   B. the curriculum focuses on formal academic training rather than unstructured play.
   C. they are funded by government agencies rather than nonprofit groups.
   D. children are placed in small groups.

5. True or False: Although findings vary, most studies indicate that children who attend preschool intervention programs like Jumpstart have higher IQ scores during their first few years of formal education. (Chapter 9, pp. 349–350)

Segment 25
Playful Learning in Early Childhood

Maureen Kelly is the director of Katie's Kids, a child-care center dedicated to the idea that young children learn best through play and exploration. She and classroom teacher Kara Klockenga explain the "project approach"—a method in which learning experiences in reading, math, science, and other areas are integrated as children engage in playful, multifaceted investigation of a single topic, selected because of children's interest in it. Maureen and the teachers also discuss the importance of play in advancing children's social skills and in preparing them for kindergarten.

For Discussion

1. Review the attributes of high-quality child care that are listed in your text. Which of these features do you notice at Katie's Kids? (Chapter 6, p. 231)

   _____

   _____

   _____

   _____

2. Briefly explain how teachers like Kara help children learn through play, noting the benefits of this approach. (Chapter 9, p. 348)

   _____

   _____

   _____

   _____

3. How does the play-based curriculum at Katie's Kids help children develop social skills? (Chapter 10, p. 373)

   _____

   _____

   _____

   _____

4. Would Vygotsky approve of the learning environment at Katie's Kids? Explain why or why not. (Chapter 9, pp. 330–332)

   _____

   _____

   _____

   _____

Test Your Understanding

1. True or False: High-quality child care can counteract the negative influences of a stressful home life. (Chapter 6, p. 230)

2. One way that preschoolers learn to regulate their feelings and understand the feelings of others is through (Chapter 10, p. 374)
   A. sociodramatic play.
   B. joint attention.
   C. parallel play.
   D. teacher-led lessons in problem-solving.

3. Play is crucial to learning because it allows preschoolers to (Chapter 10, p. 364)
   A. access autobiographical memories.
   B. try new skills without the risk of criticism and failure.
   C. learn independently, without interference from parents or peers.
   D. learn at a controlled pace.

4. True or False: During the preschool years, organized sports teams and physical education are more effective than unstructured play at honing children's gross-motor skills. (Chapter 8, p. 313)

5. In a Vygotskian classroom, children learn (Chapter 9, p. 332)
   A. through assisted discovery and peer collaboration.
   B. basic skills in reading and mathematics.
   C. by simply observing teachers and other adults.
   D. independently through a process of trial-and-error.

Segment 26
Moral Reasoning and Distributive Justice

Seven-year-old Zoe responds to a variety of scenarios designed to elicit reasoning about moral imperatives, social conventions, and matters of personal choice. She reasons rigidly about moral imperatives, providing more flexible answers to questions about social conventions and personal choices. Next, Zoe reasons about distributive justice, or how to divide material goods fairly. She responds to a scenario in which classmates must divide profits from greeting card sales. She shows an interest in strict equality, stating that the money should be distributed evenly among classmates. Her concern for all classmates, regardless of their individual sales, reveals a budding sense of benevolence.

For Discussion

1. Briefly summarize aspects of morality emphasized by the following theories. (Chapter 10, pp. 378–385)

   Psychoanalytic theory: _____

   _____

   Social learning theory: _____

   _____

   Cognitive-developmental perspective: _____

   _____

2. Explain how Zoe's personal characteristics may have contributed to her moral development. (Chapter 10, pp. 379–380)

   _____

   _____

   _____

   _____

3. Zoe judges moral violations as more wrong than violations of social conventions. How might she have arrived at this distinction? (Chapter 10, p. 385)

   _____

   _____

   _____

4. How is Zoe's awareness of personal choice likely to enhance her moral understanding? (Chapter 13, pp. 384–385)

   _____

   _____

   _____

Test Your Understanding

1. Most theories of moral development agree that at first, the child's morality is (externally/internally) controlled. Gradually, it becomes regulated by (external/internal) standards. (Chapter 10, p. 378)

2. True or False: According to social learning theory, Zoe's moral standards developed through reinforcement and modeling. (Chapter 10, p. 378)

3. According to Freud, Zoe likely adopted the moral standards of her _____ (Chapter 10, p. 378)
    A. father.
    B. mother.
    C. community.
    D. peers.

4. Parents can effectively promote moral development by _____ (Chapter 10, p. 379)
    A. using physical force.
    B. withdrawing parental love.
    C. using inductive discipline.
    D. threatening punishment.

5. (Moral imperatives/Social conventions/Matters of personal choice) are determined solely by consensus. (Chapter 10, p. 384)

Segment 27
Child Abuse

In this segment, a social worker responds to child abuse allegations. Fifteen-year-old Amber alleges that her stepfather, Cary, hit her. Although Cary claims that Amber's injuries are self-inflicted, the social worker decides to remove Amber and her two young brothers from the home. To get the boys back, Cary and Michelle, Amber's mother, agree to counseling and are subject to social workers' unannounced home visits. For a year, Amber is a ward of the state and lives with a foster family, after which she returns home. The added stress of the situation leads Cary and Michelle to divorce.

For Discussion

1. Why did the social worker decide to take all of Cary and Michelle's children out of the home? What must Cary and Michelle do to regain custody of their children?
   A. _____
   _____
   _____
   B. _____
   _____
   _____

2. List five factors associated with child maltreatment. Which of these factors are evident in the video? (Chapter 10, p. 402, Table 10.3)
   A. _____
   B. _____
   C. _____
   D. _____
   E. _____

3. If the abuse allegations are true, what consequences are Amber and her younger brothers likely to experience? Use research in the text to support your answer. (Chapter 10, pp. 403–404)
   _____
   _____
   _____
   _____

4. Briefly describe aspects of effective intervention programs aimed at preventing or reducing child maltreatment. (Chapter 10, pp. 404–405)
   _____
   _____
   _____
   _____

5. At the end of the segment, the narrator states that Amber has now experienced two divorces. What are some immediate and long-term consequences associated with parental divorce? What can Cary and Michelle do to help their children adjust favorably to their separation? (Chapter 13, p. 514)

A. _____

_____

_____

B. _____

_____

_____

Test Your Understanding

1. _____ commit more than 80 percent of abusive incidents. (Chapter 10, p. 402)
   A. Parents
   B. Strangers
   C. Adolescent boys
   D. Siblings

2. Which of the following statements about child abuse is true? (Chapter 10, p. 402)
   A. Mothers engage in sexual abuse more often than fathers.
   B. Infants and young preschoolers are at greatest risk for neglect.
   C. Fathers engage in physical abuse more often than mothers.
   D. Most sexual abuse victims are identified in adolescence.

3. True or False: Research shows that nearly all perpetrators of child abuse display an "abusive personality type." (Chapter 10, p. 402)

4. _____ is the most important factor in preventing mothers with childhood histories of abuse from repeating the cycle with their own children. (Chapter 10, p. 404)
   A. A trusting relationship with another person
   B. Extensive psychotherapy
   C. Training in effective discipline techniques
   D. Financial support

5. Which of the following statements about divorce is true? (Chapter 13, p. 512)
   A. The majority of children show improved adjustment by six months after divorce.
   B. Compared to boys, girls tend to receive less emotional support from mothers, teachers, and peers.
   C. Remaining in a high-conflict family is actually better for children than transitioning to a low-conflict, single-parent household.
   D. Remaining in a high-conflict family is worse for children than transitioning to a low-conflict, single-parent household.

Segment 28
Childhood Obesity

Two years ago, high school senior Sam Deadmond made the decision to lose weight. Today, he's proudly 50 pounds lighter and has a new perspective on making healthy lifestyle choices. In this segment, Sam and his parents discuss his struggles with his weight, the positive changes he's made to his lifestyle, and the causes and consequences of America's childhood obesity epidemic.

For Discussion

1. According to Sam, what lifestyle choices led to his obesity?

_____

_____

_____

_____

2. Describe how the entire family is helping Sam with his weight-loss goal, and explain why this approach is effective in treating obese children. (Chapter 11, pp. 419–421)
   A. _____

   _____

   B. _____

   _____

3. Explain the changes Sam has made to his lifestyle in order to lose weight. Based on research in your text about childhood obesity, do you think that Sam will be able to maintain these changes long-term? Why or why not? (Chapter 11, pp. 419–421)
   A. _____

   _____

   B. _____

   _____

4. How have Sam's weight loss and his participation in his school's ROTC program influenced his self-esteem?

_____

_____

_____

_____

Test Your Understanding

1. Early consequences of obesity that begin to appear during the school years include (Chapter 11, p. 417)
   A. high blood pressure and high cholesterol levels.
   B. type 1 diabetes and difficulty concentrating.
   C. anoxia and marasmus.
   D. myopia and ADHD.

2. Obese children are more responsive to _____ and less responsive to _____ than their average-weight agemates. (Chapter 11, p. 418)
   A. teasing from peers; social skills intervention
   B. internal hunger cues; medication
   C. physical activity; food-related words
   D. external stimuli such as taste and smell; internal hunger cues

3. True or False: A body mass index (BMI) in the 50th percentile for a child's age and sex is considered overweight, while a BMI above the 75th percentile is considered obese. (Chapter 11, p. 416)

4. Childhood obesity can be difficult to treat because (Chapter 11, p. 419)
   A. obese children have shorter attention spans than their average-weight peers.
   B. rewards for reducing sedentary time are often ineffective.
   C. it is a problem that is rooted in a family's attitudes and lifestyle.
   D. there are few weight-loss programs that focus on young people.

5. True or False: Heredity is the most influential factor in the childhood obesity epidemic. (Chapter 11, p. 417)

Segment 29
ADHD

This segment features two families that have been affected by attention-deficit hyperactivity disorder (ADHD). Kelly and Ryan describe their experiences raising 12-year-old Andrew, who was diagnosed with ADHD in early childhood. Annette, a single mother, has two boys, ages 13 and 9, with ADHD. Annette's older son, Jacob, tends to be more disorganized and inattentive, whereas her younger son, Zachary, is more hyperactive.

For Discussion

1. Cite evidence from the video that heredity plays a major role in ADHD. What environmental factors are associated with ADHD? (Chapter 12, p. 444, Biology and Environment)

   A. _____

   _____

   B. _____

   _____

2. As noted in the text, stimulant medication is the most common treatment for ADHD. What troubling side effects have Kelly, Ryan, and Annette witnessed in their children? How has medication helped Jacob and Zachary function more effectively at home and at school? (Chapter 12, p. 445, Biology and Environment)

   A. _____

   _____

   B. _____

   _____

3. Although Andrew no longer takes stimulant medication, he still needs support and guidance from his parents. What strategies do Kelly and Ryan use in lieu of medication?

   _____

   _____

   _____

4. What academic and child-rearing challenges have Kelly, Ryan, and Annette faced with their sons? How have they adjusted to these challenges? According the text, why is family intervention important in the treatment of ADHD? (Chapter 12, p. 445, Biology and Environment)

   A. _____

   _____

   B. _____

   _____

   C. _____

   _____

5. Using research in the text to support your answer, how might the behavioral characteristics of children with ADHD contribute to their peer acceptance? What interventions might be necessary to help children with ADHD interact more effectively with peers? (Chapter 13, pp. 500–503)

   A. _____

   _____

   B. _____

   _____

Test Your Understanding

1. _____ are diagnosed with ADHD about four times as often as _____. (Chapter 12, p. 444, Biology and Environment)
   A. Preschoolers; school-age children
   B. Boys; girls
   C. Girls; boys
   D. White children; black children

2. Andrew describes ADHD as a _____
   A. gift.
   B. curse.
   C. way to get attention.
   D. stigmatizing label.

3. Because of their difficulty concentrating, children with ADHD _____ (Chapter 12, p. 444, Biology and Environment)
   A. resist structure and routine.
   B. need harsh, restrictive child rearing.
   C. score 7 to 15 points lower than other children on intelligence tests.
   D. are unable to function in the regular classroom.

4. The most effective treatment approach for ADHD combines _____ (Chapter 12, p. 445, Biology and Environment)
   A. antidepressant medication, peer tutoring, and a 504 plan at school.
   B. dietary restrictions and a regular exercise routine.
   C. individual therapy with "no nonsense" discipline.
   D. medication with interventions that model and reinforce appropriate academic and social behavior.

5. True or False: ADHD is usually a lifelong disorder. (Chapter 12, p. 445, Biology and Environment)

Segment 30
Cooperative Learning

Swallowcliffe School in Adelaide, South Australia, serves mostly low-SES families. A new administration has transformed the school from a rundown, neglected state into a unique place where cooperative learning takes place at all levels. Teachers team-teach in multigrade classrooms, guiding children in acquiring cooperative learning skills, while older children tutor and support younger children. When peer difficulties arise, teachers and students come up with joint solutions through class meetings and other collaborative problem-solving techniques. Parent involvement in children's learning is central to the success of Swallowcliffe's educational program.

For Discussion

1. At Swallowcliffe School, teachers guide children in peer collaboration. What Vygotskian concepts are consistent with this approach? Explain. (Chapter 12, pp. 468–469)

   _____

   _____

   _____

2. Describe benefits of training Western children in collaborative processes. (Chapter 12, p. 471)

   _____

   _____

   _____

3. Describe outcomes associated with homogeneous grouping in elementary school. (Chapter 12, p. 470)

   _____

   _____

   _____

4. Cite outcomes associated with placement in multigrade classrooms, such as those at Swallowcliffe School. (Chapter 12, p. 470)

   _____

   _____

   _____

5. Swallowcliffe School makes a concerted effort to involve parents in their children's education. How can parent involvement benefit students and families? (Chapter 12, pp. 582–583)

   _____

   _____

   _____

Test Your Understanding

1. According to Vygotsky, _____ can spur children's learning. (Chapter 12, p. 469)
   A. only teachers
   B. only more expert peers
   C. only independent exploration
   D. both teachers and more expert peers

2. True or False: Children profit more from cooperative learning when their partner is an "expert"—especially capable at the task. (Chapter 12, p. 471)

3. Teaching through cooperative learning broadens Vygotsky's concept of _____ (Chapter 12, p. 471)
   A. private speech.
   B. the zone of proximal development.
   C. egocentric speech
   D. children as naïve theorists.

4. Academic achievement, self-esteem, and attitudes toward school are usually more favorable in (multigrade/single-grade) classrooms. (Chapter 12, p. 470)

5. True or False: American children usually do not require training in cooperative learning and collaborative practices, due to the collectivist nature of Western society. (Chapter 12, p. 471)

Segment 31
First-Grade Science Education

Stacy Holzwarth, a first-grade teacher at Chicago's Nettelhorst School, uses music to set the rhythm for the day and to draw her students into the process of learning. Her science lessons emphasize collaboration, exploration, and independent discovery. She invites the children to "think like scientists" as they investigate samples of algae and share their findings with their classmates.

For Discussion

1. How does Stacy use music and physical movement in her classroom? Describe how the children respond to the music as the lesson begins.
   A. _____
   _____
   _____
   B. _____
   _____
   _____

2. Using examples from the video and research presented in the text, how has Stacy created a community of learners? (Chapter 12, p. 469)
   _____
   _____
   _____

3. How does working in small groups make learning more effective in this science lesson? (Chapter 12, pp. 470–471)
   _____
   _____
   _____

4. Explain how Stacy brings small groups of students back together to discuss their findings at the end of the lesson. How does she encourage the groups to share what they've learned?
   _____
   _____
   _____

5. What strategies does Stacy use to promote high-level thinking among her students?
   _____
   _____
   _____
   _____

Test Your Understanding

1. In an educational approach known as _____, small groups of students work together to solve problems, compare ideas, and guide each other's understanding of concepts. (Chapter 12, p. 471)

2. True or False: The philosophy of Stacy's classroom is best described as traditional, in that the teacher is the sole authority for knowledge and decision making. (Chapter 12, p. 467)

3. Teachers who create _____ believe that both teachers and students should work together in joint endeavors, with no distinction between adult and child contributors. (Chapter 12, p. 469)
   A. traditional learning environments
   B. Piagetian classrooms
   C. self-fulfilling prophecies
   D. communities of learners

4. True or False: The concept of a "community of learners" is an elaboration on Vygotsky's zone of proximal development, encouraging collaboration between students and more expert peers. (Chapter 12, p. 469)

5. Stacy applies the Piagetian educational principle of _____ as she encourages her students to closely examine their samples of algae. (Chapter 9, pp. 328–329)
   A. proximal development
   B. discovery learning
   C. knowledge construction
   D. cognitive mapping

Segment 32
Dramatic Arts Education

Chad Kimmel teaches drama to elementary and middle-school students at Chicago's Nettelhorst School. He focuses on making the younger children comfortable with their own bodies and open to the possibilities of creative movement. His middle-school students write and perform monologues, act in plays, and even direct scenes. He says that arts education helps young people acquire discipline, self-expression, and confidence.

For Discussion

1. Using research on gross- and fine-motor development in preschoolers, how might Chad's classes facilitate motor development in his younger students? (Chapter 8, pp. 313–314)

   _____

   _____

   _____

   _____

2. How might Chad's classes nurture children's creativity? Provide specific examples. (Chapter 12, pp. 474–475)

   _____

   _____

   _____

   _____

3. How does dramatic arts education enhance self-esteem during middle childhood? (Chapter 13, pp. 485–488)

   _____

   _____

   _____

   _____

4. Chad says that drama classes can help children learn discipline and self-regulation. Provide evidence that supports this claim. (Chapter 13, pp. 490–491)

   _____

   _____

   _____

   _____

Test Your Understanding

1. During the preschool years, children like Chad's youngest students (Chapter 8, p. 308)
   A. typically lag behind in development of fine-motor skills, while showing gains in gross-motor skills.
   B. require extensive, regimented training in music and the arts to encourage later creativity.
   C. become frustrated by their inability to perform simple self-care tasks.
   D. enjoy learning new motor skills and mastering control of their own bodies.

2. Dramatic arts education, such as that depicted in the video, encourages development of _____. (Chapter 12, p. 474)
   A. creativity
   B. analytical problem solving
   C. moral self-relevance
   D. general intelligence

3. True or False: Self-esteem and feelings of competence typically decrease as children enter the school years. (Chapter 13, p. 484)

4. True or False: Drama lessons for young children have been found to boost intelligence test scores, similar to the famed "Mozart effect." (Chapter 1, p. 44, Social Issues)

5. Training that encourages discipline and self-regulation helps children develop _____, crediting their successes to their own ability and hard work. (Chapter 13, p. 486)
   A. achievement-related attributions
   B. creativity
   C. mastery-oriented attributions
   D. learned helplessness

Segment 33
Revitalizing an Inner-City School

Eight years ago, Nettelhorst School in inner-city Chicago was a bleak, forbidding building filled with discouraged teachers and troubled students bused in from other overcrowded schools. Today, Nettelhorst is a vibrant, enriching environment where students from many different walks of life learn together in innovative ways. Jacqueline Edelberg, who spearheaded the effort to transform Nettelhorst, explains how a group of dedicated neighborhood parents succeeded in revitalizing the school. Principal Cindy Wulbert discusses what makes Nettelhorst so successful, while parent leaders talk about the challenges that Nettelhorst faces today.

For Discussion

1. Describe the condition of Nettelhorst when Jacqueline and her fellow parents first visited the school. How might such an environment encourage educational self-fulfilling prophecies? (Chapter 12, p. 470)

   A. _____

   _____

   _____

   B. _____

   _____

   _____

2. How did Jacqueline and other Nettelhorst parents work to transform the school? Provide specific examples from the video.

   _____

   _____

   _____

3. How does Nettelhorst forge bonds among students, the school, and parents?

   _____

   _____

   _____

4. Explain what the principal, Cindy, means when she mentions the "achievement gap." Why do you think Nettelhorst has been effective in narrowing that gap? (Chapter 12, pp. 458–461, 470, 471)

   A. _____

   _____

   _____

   B. _____

   _____

   _____

5. Nettelhorst is designated a magnet school specializing in the arts. Explain what this means. (Chapter 12, p. 471, Social Issues)

_____

_____

_____

Test Your Understanding

1. One of the major problems that Jacqueline sought to fix at the "old" Nettelhorst was overcrowding. Small class sizes are beneficial because (Chapter 12, p. 467)
   A. there are fewer disruptive children in smaller classrooms.
   B. teachers are able to spend more time on instruction and less time on discipline.
   C. teachers are able to isolate children with discipline problems.
   D. rote instruction is easier with fewer children.

2. True or False: Ethnic and SES segregation in U.S. schools leads to homogenous grouping, in which low-SES, minority students decline in self-esteem and motivation. (Chapter 12, p. 470)

3. The establishment of _____ in urban areas decreases the impact of ethnic and SES segregation by attracting students from surrounding neighborhoods and more affluent parts of the city. (Chapter 12, p. 471, Social Issues)
   A. community schools
   B. Head Start centers
   C. magnet schools
   D. Montessori schools

4. True or False: Quality after-school programs like those offered at Nettelhorst can help improve academic performance and social skills for children who live in impoverished neighborhoods. (Chapter 2, p. 76)

5. Parent involvement in schools, especially in low-income areas, is crucial because (Chapter 15, p. 583)
   A. it teaches children that their parents value education.
   B. teachers in inner-city schools often do not encourage parent participation.
   C. there is less time for classroom instruction in inner-city schools.
   D. it encourages residents who don't have children in the school to get involved.

Name _____

Date _____

Segment 34
School–Community Partnership

Students at Nettelhorst School are able to take advantage of a thriving community school program that offers classes and other learning experiences outside of usual school hours. Instructors from the community help forge connections between families and the neighborhood, while students benefit from a safe, constructive environment after school. In this segment, the community school director and teachers talk about what makes their program so effective, while the school's principal discusses the importance of opening the doors of Nettelhorst to the community.

For Discussion

1. Think about what you've learned about high-quality elementary school classrooms. Which of the characteristics of these classrooms are evident in the after-school programs at Jane's Place? Provide specific examples. (Chapter 12, p. 467)

   _____

   _____

   _____

   _____

2. How might the partnership between Nettelhorst and the community affect children's development? Consider the importance of the neighborhood in urban children's lives. (Chapter 2, p. 76)

   _____

   _____

   _____

   _____

3. How is exposure to new skills and ideas likely to benefit community school participants' social and emotional development? (Chapter 10, pp. 368–369)

   _____

   _____

   _____

4. Why is it so crucial that children have a place to go after the school day is over? (Chapter 13, pp. 516–517)

   _____

   _____

   _____

Test Your Understanding

1. Ties between the family and the neighborhood, promoted by programs like Jane's Place, enhance child development by (Chapter 2, p. 76)
    A. promoting social support for both parents and children.
    B. providing financial assistance.
    C. serving the same role as the extended family.
    D. reducing the impact of peers on children's lives.

2. Programs that encourage physical activity, like the Jane's Place yoga class, are especially beneficial because (Chapter 11, p. 425)
    A. Nettelhorst School does not offer recess periods for its students.
    B. exercise is more important for school-age children than for adolescents.
    C. during middle childhood, children develop behaviors that foster good health throughout the lifespan.
    D. inner-city children often lag behind in gross-motor skills.

3. True or False: Neighborhood resources have an equal impact on high-SES and low-SES families. (Chapter 2, p. 76)

4. True or False: Integration of academic subjects with music, art, and physical education is key to a high-quality elementary curriculum. (Chapter 12, p. 467)

5. Without access to high-quality education, such as that provided by Nettelhorst, many low-SES, ethnic minority students (Chapter 15, p. 587)
    A. are at-risk for high school dropout.
    B. develop a foreclosed identity status.
    C. are forced to attend magnet schools.
    D. are assigned to low-quality multigrade classrooms.

Name _____
Date _____

Segment 35
Self-Concept in Childhood and Adolescence

The self-descriptions of 7-year-old Zoe and 15-year-old Lisa depict the development of self-concept, from concrete characteristics and typical emotions to personality traits. Five-year-old Claire and 7-year-old Liesl play a game that reveals gains in perspective taking during the early school years. The importance of social experiences—in particular, the guidance of parents and teachers—in children's social understanding is emphasized. Jean, Phil, and Carla, high school seniors, combine their various personality traits into an organized self-concept and discuss their efforts to construct an identity.

For Discussion

1. Are self-descriptions like Zoe's more characteristic of early or middle childhood? Explain. (Chapter 10, p. 365; Chapter 13, pp. 482–483)

   _____
   _____
   _____

2. How can parents help children develop a clear, optimistic self-concept? (Chapter 13, p. 483)

   _____
   _____
   _____

3. Lisa states, "I'm a pretty good student." What development paves the way for such evaluative self-descriptions? (Chapter 13, p. 483)

   _____
   _____
   _____

4. How are Leisl's perspective-taking skills likely to affect her social interactions? (Chapter 13, p. 483)

   _____
   _____
   _____

5. How do the self-descriptions of teenagers like Jean, Phil, and Carla reflect changes in self-concept during adolescence? (Chapter 16, p. 601)

   _____
   _____
   _____

Test Your Understanding

1. True or False: According to follow-up research on preoperational thought, Claire's incomplete mastery of the perspective-taking task is due to egocentrism. (Chapter 9, p. 323)

2. When recalling personally significant past experiences, Chinese children are more likely than U.S. children to _____ (Chapter 13, p. 483)
   A. include opinions.
   B. list personal attributes.
   C. give longer accounts.
   D. refer to others.

3. What does Lisa's use of a qualifier in the phrase, "I am pretty outgoing," probably reveal about her cognitive development? (Chapter 16, p. 601)
   A. She is struggling with an identity crisis.
   B. She is aware that psychological qualities can vary across situations.
   C. She does not feel pressured to display multiple selves.
   D. She may be unaware of inconsistencies in her traits.

4. How can Carla's parents best help her to develop a healthy sense of autonomy? (Chapter 16, pp. 620–621)
   A. Encourage Carla to idealize authority figures.
   B. Use coercion to guide Carla's development.
   C. Permit Carla to explore ideas and social roles.
   D. Discourage Carla from making decisions independently.

5. True or False: Consistent with Phil's experience, it is common for crowds to decline in importance by late adolescence. (Chapter 16, p. 627)

Segment 36
Peer Harassment

This segment features two high school students, 15-year-old Betsy and 16-year-old Kayla, who have both experienced peer harassment. Kayla has been bullied since elementary school, when she says her weight made her an easy target. She discusses how bullying has made it difficult for her to form a homosexual dating relationship. Betsy, once a victim of peer harassment, is now dedicated to helping others. She intervenes when she witnesses harassment and reaches out with an anti-bullying website. Guidance counselor Camille Taylor discusses the effects of bullying, common traits of bullies and their victims, and the complex task of preventing peer harassment at school.

For Discussion

1. Using research in the text and Camille's discussion, what are some characteristics of victimized children? (Chapter 13, p. 502, Biology and Environment)

_____
_____
_____

2. Describe adjustment difficulties Betsy and Kayla may face as a result of being victimized. (Chapter 13, p. 502, Biology and Environment)

_____
_____
_____

3. How are other victims of peer harassment at Betsy's school likely to benefit from her friendship? (Chapter 13, p. 502, Biology and Environment)

_____
_____
_____

4. Describe characteristics of interventions that may reduce bullying at Kayla and Betsy's school. (Chapter 13, p. 502, Biology and Environment)

_____
_____
_____

5. How do Kayla's dating experiences compare with research on gay and lesbian youths presented in your text? Explain. (Chapter 14, pp. 552–554)

_____
_____
_____

Test Your Understanding

1. About 20 to 40 percent of young people report that they have experienced _____ through text messages, e-mail, or social networking web sites. (Chapter 13, p. 502, Biology and Environment)

2. True or False: Research supports Kayla's assertion that most bullies are boys. (Chapter 13, p. 502, Biology and Environment)

3. The best way to reduce bullying is to _____ (Chapter 13, p. 502, Biology and Environment)
   A. implement zero tolerance policies in all public schools.
   B. help victimized children form and maintain a gratifying friendship.
   C. promote prosocial attitudes and behaviors in youth environments.
   D. allow victims to confront bullies without school intervention.

4. True or False: Research shows that, like Kayla, most gay, lesbian, and bisexual youths have experienced verbal abuse. (Chapter 14, p. 553, Social Issues)

5. Camille explains that Kayla and Betsy's high school is largely divided into crowds. As students mature, these crowds are likely to _____ (Chapter 16, p. 627)
   A. increase in importance.
   B. decline in importance.
   C. expand in unfavorable directions.
   D. become increasingly hostile.

Segment 37
Divorce and Father Custody

This segment features 24-year-old Bill, a custodial parent of two sons: Dylan, age 5, and Jeremy, age 4, who was born with cerebral palsy—a major disability. Bill describes the emotional pain of his divorce and why he took custody of Dylan and Jeremy. Bill is devoted to maximizing quality time with his sons. He also hopes to have the financial stability to offer Jeremy a secure future.

For Discussion

1. How are 4-year-old Jeremy and 5-year-old Dylan's age and sex likely to influence their immediate reactions to the divorce? (Chapter 13, pp. 511–512)

   Age: _____

   _____

   _____

   Sex: _____

   _____

   _____

2. Cite some long-term consequences that children of divorced parents, such as Dylan and Jeremy, often experience. What factors can reduce the likelihood that they will encounter these difficulties? (Chapter 13, p. 512)

   A. _____

   _____

   B. _____

   _____

3. How are Bill's sons likely to benefit from the sustained, affectionate involvement of a custodial father? (Chapter 13, p. 512)

   _____

   _____

   _____

4. Bill describes how parenthood, especially the arrival of a second child with disabilities, weakened his marriage. Cite factors that can ease a stressful transition to parenthood. (Chapter 4, p. 156)

   _____

   _____

   _____

Test Your Understanding

1. Cerebral palsy is caused by _____ (Chapter 4, pp. 135–136)
    A. genetic mutations during meiosis.
    B. exposure to lead-based paint during childhood.
    C. brain damage before, during, or just after birth.
    D. severe malnutrition in infancy.

2. Bill is likely to express (less/more) caring and affection for his sons than a father who spends less time near his children. (Chapter 7, p. 276)

3. The percentage of children who live in father-headed households after their parents' divorce has _____ (Chapter 13, p. 510)
    A. gradually declined.
    B. remained roughly constant.
    C. increased steadily.
    D. risen sharply.

4. True or False: If Bill remarries, his sons are likely to react positively. (Chapter 13, p. 513)

5. In Western cultures, paternal attachment _____ (Chapter 7, p. 276)
    A. protects children from emotional and behavioral problems.
    B. has less impact on development than maternal attachment.
    C. is more important than in non-Western cultures.
    D. increases in middle childhood and adolescence.

Segment 38
Homosexuality

In this segment, 24-year-old Mark describes how an unsupportive high school atmosphere in a small town made it difficult for him to accept his same-sex attraction. Mark also discusses family members' positive reactions to his coming out. Supportive relationships have helped Mark integrate his sexual orientation into a broader sense of identity and to formulate positive goals for the future.

For Discussion

1. Describe factors that made it difficult for Mark to come to terms with his sexual orientation.

   _____
   _____
   _____

2. Cite indicators that Mark has reached the self-acceptance phase of coming out to himself and others. (Chapter 14, p. 553, Biology and Environment)

   _____
   _____
   _____

3. What aspects of Mark's self-development were likely strengthened by family members' positive responses to the disclosure of his sexual orientation? (Chapter 14, p. 553, Biology and Environment)

   _____
   _____
   _____

4. Cite genetic factors and elements of the prenatal environment that may have influenced Mark's sexual orientation. (Chapter 14, p. 552)
   Genetic factors: _____

   Prenatal environment: _____
   _____

5. Would Erikson say that Mark has successfully solved the conflict of identity versus role confusion? Why or why not? (Chapter 16, p. 600)

   _____
   _____
   _____

Test Your Understanding

1. In adolescence, some gay, lesbian, and bisexual young people explore _____ activities in order to conceal knowledge of their homosexuality. (Chapter 14, p. 553, Biology and Environment)
   A. extracurricular
   B. gender-stereotyped
   C. religious
   D. non-gender-traditional

2. Gay, lesbian, and bisexual children's first sense of their biologically determined sexual orientation typically occurs in their _____ (Chapter 14, p. 553, Biology and Environment)
   A. social interactions.
   B. sexual attractions.
   C. clothing preferences.
   D. play interests.

3. Gay and bisexual boys tend to become aware of their same-sex physical attraction (earlier/later) than lesbian and bisexual girls. (Chapter 14, p. 553, Biology and Environment)

4. True or False: Most gay, lesbian, and bisexual adolescents crystallize a sexual identity quickly, in a flash of insight. (Chapter 14, p. 553, Biology and Environment)

5. True or False: Like Mark, most homosexuals do not appear "gender-deviant" in their dress or behavior. (Chapter 14, p. 552)

Segment 39
Adolescent Parenthood

When adolescents become sexually active, the consequences can be profound, as the story of 18-year-olds Rhiannon and Joel reveals. After dating Joel for a year, Rhiannon discovered that she was pregnant. Joel and Rhiannon share their reactions to the pregnancy and describe how the arrival of their son, Jacob, has changed their lives. Ray and Laurie, Joel's parents, relate their concerns about the effects of adolescent parenthood on their son's future.

For Discussion

1. Describe the potential consequences of adolescent parenthood for Joel and Rhiannon. (Chapter 14, pp. 556–557)

   _____
   _____
   _____
   _____

2. What outcomes is Jacob likely to face as the child of an adolescent mother? (Chapter 14, p. 557; p. 558, Social Issues: Health)

   _____
   _____
   _____
   _____

3. Cite several steps Rhiannon can take to minimize long-term disruptions in her own and her child's development. (Chapter 14, p. 559)

   _____
   _____
   _____
   _____

4. Both Rhiannon and Joel have parents who have supported them and participated in the rearing of Jacob. How does family support contribute to the well-being of teenage parents and their children? Explain. (Chapter 14, p. 559)

   _____
   _____
   _____
   _____

5. Although Joel and Rhiannon decided not to marry, both have taken on the responsibilities of parenthood. What is distinctive about Joel's response to parenthood? How is Joel's involvement likely to affect his son? (Chapter 14, p. 559)

A. _____

_____

B. _____

_____

Test Your Understanding

1. True or False: Teenage mothers' physical immaturity often results in prenatal complications. (Chapter 3, p. 116)

2. True or False: Like Joel, most adolescent parents come from well-educated, middle-class families. (Chapter 14, p. 556)

3. As an adolescent mother, Rhiannon is more likely to _____ than her agemates who postpone childbearing. (Chapter 14, p. 556)
   A. parent warmly
   B. marry
   C. divorce
   D. obtain a satisfying, well-paying job

4. The child of adolescent parents, Jacob is less likely to _____ than children from other families. (Chapter 14, p. 557)
   A. perform poorly in school
   B. graduate from high school
   C. engage in disruptive social behavior
   D. become an adolescent parent himself

5. The most difficult and costly way to deal with adolescent pregnancy is to _____ (Chapter 14, p. 559)
   A. provide adolescents with contraceptive services.
   B. foster academic and social competence in at-risk adolescents.
   C. provide comprehensive sex education for all adolescents.
   D. delay interventions until adolescent pregnancy occurs.

Segment 40
Adolescent Friendship

Best friends Mari, age 13, and Sarah, age 14, talk about the meaning and importance of friendship in adolescence. They discuss relationship qualities that have enabled their friendship to blossom and endure. While Mari and Sarah are from different ethnic backgrounds, they describe several key personality similarities that have drawn them together. Mari and Sarah also share their observations of sex and ethnic differences in friendships. The interview concludes with the friends' thoughts on romantic relationships with the opposite sex.

For Discussion

1. Explain how Mari and Sarah's close friendship is likely to ease their transition from junior high school to high school. (Chapter 15, p. 581)

   _____
   _____
   _____

2. Describe how Mari and Sarah's relationship reflects the three important characteristics of adolescent friendship discussed in the text. (Chapter 16, pp. 622–623)
   Intimacy: _____
   _____
   Mutual understanding: _____
   _____
   Loyalty: _____
   _____

3. When forming friendships, adolescents often judge commonality in certain attributes as more important than in others. Which commonalities appear more important to Mari and Sarah? Which appear less important to them?
   A. _____
   _____
   B. _____
   _____

4. How do Mari and Sarah's observations of sex differences in friendships compare with those mentioned in the text? (Chapter 16, p. 624)

   _____
   _____
   _____
   _____

5. From what you have observed of Sarah and Mari's personal qualities, in what ways are the girls likely to benefit from their friendship? (Chapter 16, pp. 625–626)

    _____

    _____

    _____

    _____

Test Your Understanding

1. True or False: As a result of their close, cross-race friendship, Sarah and Mari are less likely to hold subtle, unintentional prejudices. (Chapter 13, p. 497)

2. Self-disclosure (declines/remains constant/increases) over the adolescent years. (Chapter 16, p. 623)

3. Mari and Sarah most likely get together to _____ (Chapter 16, p. 624)
    A. "just talk."
    B. coruminate.
    C. gossip and compete with one another.
    D. participate in family activities.

4. Which of the following statements about sex differences in friendships is true? (Chapter 16, p. 624)
    A. Girls' friendships typically focus on achievement and status.
    B. Girls' friendships typically focus on communal concerns.
    C. "Masculine" boys are just as likely as girls to form intimate same-sex ties.
    D. Gender identity has little or no effect on friendship ties.

5. True or False: Girls' closest same-sex friendships tend to be of longer duration than boys'. (Chapter 16, p. 624)

Segment 41
Adolescent Dating

In this segment, 18-year-old Mike and 17-year-old Haley describe their dating relationship, including how they first met, why they were attracted to each other, and their future plans. Although Mike and Haley had previous dating experiences, this relationship marked the first serious commitment for each of them. They explain why they do not mind attending separate high schools and elaborate on their plans to attend separate colleges.

For Discussion

1. How do strong friendships prepare adolescents for future romantic relationships? (Chapter 16, p. 626)

   _____

   _____

   _____

2. Haley discusses how her criteria for a dating partner have changed over time. According to your text, is this progression typical? Explain. (Chapter 16, p. 627)

   _____

   _____

   _____

3. Explain how attachment to parents and caregivers contributes to close relationships in adolescence. (Chapter 16, pp. 627–628)

   _____

   _____

   _____

4. Describe the benefits of adolescent dating. (Chapter 16, p. 628)

   _____

   _____

   _____

5. Based on their discussion, if Haley and Mike's relationship continues into early adulthood, is it likely to be mutually satisfying and long-lasting? Explain, citing evidence from your text. (Chapter 16, p. 628)

   _____

   _____

   _____

   _____

Test Your Understanding

1. Of the following, which statement about adolescent dating is true? (Chapter 16, p. 627)
   A. The hormonal changes of puberty determine when and how dating begins.
   B. Young adolescents' romantic relationships last, on average, for nearly two years.
   C. Asian youths start dating later than young people in Western societies.
   D. Asian youths have more dating partners than Western adolescents.

2. Early dating in adolescence is related to _____ (Chapter 16, p. 628)
   A. drug use, delinquency, and poor academic achievement.
   B. greater social maturity and high academic achievement.
   C. advanced moral reasoning and decreased likelihood of dating violence.
   D. high self-esteem, more friends, and closer relationships with parents.

3. Compared with heterosexual relationships like Haley and Mike's, gay and lesbian dating relationships in adolescence tend to _____ (Chapter 16, p. 628)
   A. last longer.
   B. involve greater emotional commitment.
   C. be easier to initiate.
   D. involve greater fear of harassment and peer rejection.

4. As long as it does not begin too soon, adolescent dating _____ (Chapter 16, p. 628)
   A. contributes to popularity and social status.
   B. remains superficial but helps build self-esteem.
   C. contributes to later age of first marriage.
   D. improves social skills and cooperation.

5. True or False: When heterosexual adolescent romances survive high school graduation, partner satisfaction tends to be high. (Chapter 16, p. 628)

Segment 42
Civic Engagement in Adolescence

Allysa Grayson is a college-bound high school senior who has faced many challenges, including being raised by a single mother in a poverty-stricken neighborhood. But Allysa's commitment to community service and her involvement in extracurricular activities at her school have honed her leadership skills and determination to succeed. Now, her goals are to finish college and inspire other young people, including her three siblings, to work hard and set goals for their futures.

For Discussion

1. Define civic responsibility. What attributes of civic responsibility does Allysa display? (Chapter 16, p. 616, Social Issues)

   Definition: _____

   _____

   Allysa: _____

   _____

2. Review the concept of resilience along with factors that promote it. How does Allysa's story reflect her personal resilience? (Chapter 1, pp. 10–11, Biology and Environment)

   _____

   _____

   _____

   _____

3. How might Allysa's participation in extracurricular activities have helped her overcome the challenges she faced? (Chapter 15, p. 589)

   _____

   _____

   _____

   _____

4. As a first-generation college student from a low-SES family, how can Allysa's university help her adjust to campus life and reduce the risk of dropout during the first year? (Chapter 17, p. 653)

   _____

   _____

   _____

Test Your Understanding

1. Research confirms that family, school, and community influences contribute to the development of _____ in young people, leading them to express a commitment to working toward societal goals. (Chapter 16, p. 616, Social Issues)
   A. religiosity
   B. resilience
   C. civic responsibility
   D. moral development

2. Strong relationships with _____ are crucial in high school and emerging adulthood, promoting high self-esteem, academic achievement, and reduced anxiety.
   (Chapter 17, p. 657)
   A. siblings
   B. parents
   C. community members
   D. teachers and mentors

3. True or False: The desire to contribute meaningfully to one's community is one attribute of resilience in emerging adulthood. (Chapter 17, p. 657)

4. Participation in _____ encourages academic improvement, higher self-esteem, and reduced antisocial behavior in high school students. (Chapter 15, p. 589)
   A. unstructured leisure-time activities
   B. team athletics
   C. support groups
   D. extracurricular activities

5. True or False: Contemporary first-year students enrolled in U.S. college and universities are more likely than those of a decade ago to expect to participate in community service, and most who intend to participate actually do so. (Chapter 17, p. 655)

Name _____

Date _____

Segment 43
Changing Parent-Adolescent Relationships

This segment features Bob and Teresa and their 12-year-old daughter, Izzy. As she enters adolescence, Izzy's attitude toward her parents has changed, and their discussions frequently erupt into arguments. Izzy is particularly upset by her parents' rules about Internet use and longs for more privacy. Meanwhile, Bob and Teresa wish their daughter would show them more respect.

For Discussion

1. As young people enter adolescence, they often deidealize their parents. Provide examples from the video that support this statement. (Chapter 16, p. 619)

_____

_____

_____

_____

2. What are the main issues that spark disagreement between Izzy and her parents? How do these issues reflect Izzy's growing need for autonomy? (Chapter 16, p. 619)
   A. _____
   B. _____

_____

_____

3. Citing examples from the video, how would you describe the child-rearing style used by Bob and Teresa? (Chapter 10, pp. 398–400)

_____

_____

_____

_____

4. Izzy believes that her parents are purposefully trying to embarrass her. How does this attitude reflect the cognitive changes of adolescence? (Chapter 15, p. 572)

_____

_____

_____

_____

Test Your Understanding

1. Effective parenting of adolescents strikes a balance between _____ and _____. (Chapter 16, p. 619)
   A. control; discipline
   B. connection; separation
   C. coercion; control
   D. autonomy; acceptance

2. Assume that Izzy becomes sarcastic and crtical toward her parents while on a shopping trip. According to research in the text, what is the best way for Izzy's parents to deal with her behavior? (Chaper 15, p. 572)
   A. Address the problem immediately when it happens to avoid the likelihood of it recurring.
   B. Wait until they can speak to Izzy alone, and address the problem then.
   C. Ignore the behavior and hope that it will disappear as Izzy matures.
   D. Have another respected adult, like a teacher or counselor, deal with the behavior.

3. True or False: The quality of the parent-child relationship is the best predictor of mental well-being during adolescence. (Chapter 16, p. 621)

4. True or False: For most young people, conflict with parents does not lessen until the end of the college years. (Chapter 16, p. 621)

5. Adolescents are often embarrassed by their parents' behavior because of a cognitive distortion known as the _____, the belief that they are the focus of others' attention and concern. (Chapter 15, p. 572)
   A. imaginary audience
   B. egocentric idealism
   C. personal fable
   D. role confusion

Segment 44
Delinquency

Thirteen-year-old Joshua was removed from his mother and stepfather's home after an alleged violent outburst. This segment follows Joshua through the juvenile court system, from being charged with battery to spending a month in an emergency shelter. After being declared a ward of the state, he is sent to a juvenile facility for one year. Joshua discusses how his parents' divorce affected him and why he is reluctant to return to his family.

For Discussion

1. Describe discipline practices that might have helped Joshua develop better self-control and conduct. (Chapter 10, pp. 379, 381–384)

   _____
   _____
   _____

2. Summarize three reasons why boys tend to be more physically aggressive than girls. (Chapter 10, p. 386)
   A. _____
   B. _____
   C. _____

3. Describe how cyclical, conflict-ridden parent–child interaction may have promoted Joshua's aggressive behavior. (Chapter 10, p. 387)

   _____
   _____
   _____

4. How could Joshua's parents have protected their son from negative, long-term consequences of divorce? (Chapter 13, pp. 512–513)

   _____
   _____
   _____

5. Describe characteristics of a treatment program that might effectively reduce Joshua's delinquent behavior. (Chapter 16, p. 635)

   _____
   _____
   _____

Test Your Understanding

1. When Joshua responded angrily and violently to his mother's discipline, he was engaging in _____ aggression. (Chapter 10, p. 385)
   A. proactive
   B. reactive
   C. indirect physical
   D. direct relational

2. Joshua believes he would fare better if his biological father was awarded custody. Research (supports/refutes) Joshua's speculation. (Chapter 13, p. 512)

3. Which of the following is true of mother–stepfather blended families? (Chapter 13, p. 514)
   A. Like Joshua, boys tend to adjust poorly to the addition of a stepfather.
   B. Mother–son friction tends to increase as the result of remarriage.
   C. Mother–son friction tends to decrease as the result of remarriage.
   D. Girls tend to adjust more easily to mother–stepfather families than boys.

4. Which of the following is true about adolescent delinquency? (Chapter 16, p. 634)
   A. Youth crime has increased in the U.S. since the mid-1990s.
   B. For most adolescents, a brush with the law does not forecast long-term antisocial behavior.
   C. Rates of delinquency remain roughly constant throughout the teenage years.
   D. As peers become more influential in late adolescence, delinquency increases.

5. True or False: Boys who experience parental separation and divorce are especially prone to delinquency. (Chapter 16, p. 634)

Name _____

Date _____

Segment 45
Identity and Emerging Adulthood

This segment opens with 25-year-old Casey discussing her identity and dreams for the future. Casey has entered a period of development called emerging adulthood; she has left adolescence but has not yet fully assumed adult responsibilities. Casey's graduate-level studies have helped her to form an independent identity and select a career path. Next, 24-year-old Elizabeth and 25-year-old Joel discuss the transition to adulthood. Although Elizabeth and Joel have both graduated from college and obtained full-time jobs, they do not feel as though they have fully reached adulthood. They describe how they will know that they have attained this milestone.

For Discussion

1. What factors may help Casey, Elizabeth, and Joel to overcome the stressors and risks of emerging adulthood? (Chapter 17, p. 657)

   _____

   _____

2. What factors have contributed to Casey's identity development? Are these factors consistent with research presented in the text? Explain. (Chapter 17, pp. 649–652)

   A. _____

   _____

   B. _____

   _____

3. What markers of adulthood do Elizabeth and Joel mention? Are their responses typical for their age group? Explain. (Chapter 17, p. 645)

   A. _____

   _____

   B. _____

   _____

4. How do Casey, Elizabeth, and Joel's dreams compare with Levinson's research on constructing a dream in emerging adulthood? Explain. (Chapter 17, p. 652)

   _____

   _____

   _____

5. As women and/or ethnic minorities, Casey, Joel, and Elizabeth are likely to face career struggles. Cite several factors that may help them to surmount these challenges. (Chapter 17, pp. 653–654)

   _____

   _____

   _____

Test Your Understanding

1. Casey describes the transition from closely following her parents' beliefs to constructing a more flexible belief system and following her own "truth." She has likely moved from _____ thinking to _____ thinking. (Chapter 17, p. 648)

2. Casey is most likely to advance her epistemic cognition if she _____ (Chapter 17, p. 648)
   A. encounters challenges to her perspective.
   B. tackles unrealistic problems.
   C. solves challenging problems independently.
   D. enlists the help of more expert partners when faced with a challenge.

3. True or False: Casey would likely have experienced less cognitive growth if she had opted not to attend college. (Chapter 17, p. 649)

4. Casey has chosen to work in the field of gerontology and is experimenting before she settles on a single occupation within her field. Casey is likely in the _____ period of vocational development. (Chapter 15, p. 591)
   A. fantasy
   B. tentative
   C. realistic
   D. exploration

5. Which of the following has contributed to emerging adulthood? (Chapter 17, pp. 644–645)
   A. declining enrollment in higher education
   B. slight declines in life expectancy in prosperous nations
   C. pressing needs for young people's labor
   D. delays in financial independence and career commitment

Segment 46
Resilience: From Gang Member to Responsible Adult

Eighteen-year-old Julio grew up in a poverty-stricken Chicago neighborhood and, seeking an escape from his abusive home life, became involved in gang violence at an early age. When his family moved to a smaller city, Julio seized the opportunity to turn his life around. Now a college student, Julio reflects on the turmoil of his childhood and talks about personal qualities and external influences that have made him resilient. Still, Julio faces continuing challenges.

For Discussion

1. Review four broad factors that influence resilience, as listed in your text. How did these factors influence Julio's life? (Chapter 1, pp. 10–11, Biology and Environment)

   _____

   _____

   _____

2. Why did Julio turn to gang life? How does this relate to what you have learned about delinquent behavior in adolescence? (Chapter 16, pp. 633–635)

   _____

   _____

   _____

   _____

3. Julio says that he struggles to control his aggression. What characteristics of his childhood and family life might have contributed to his hostility and aggression? (Chapter 10, p. 387)

   _____

   _____

   _____

   _____

4. Would you consider Julio an "emerging adult"? Why or why not? (Chapter 17, pp. 644–645)

   _____

   _____

   _____

   _____

Test Your Understanding

1. One of the most important contributors to children's resilience is (Chapter 1, p. 11)
   A. residence in a middle-class neighborhood.
   B. early intervention by social workers and an academically challenging preschool.
   C. a strong bond to a competent, caring, adult either within or outside the family.
   D. warm relationships with older siblings.

2. Neighborhood resources have a greater impact on _____ than on _____ children. (Chapter 2, p. 76)
   A. highly-motivated; delinquent
   B. high-SES; low-SES
   C. resilient; nonresilient
   D. low-SES; high-SES

3. Aggressive behavior in children is often rooted in (Chapter 10, p. 387)
   A. a conflict-ridden family atmosphere and forceful discipline.
   B. overly permissive parenting.
   C. hereditary factors.
   D. lack of empathy and difficulty understanding moral imperatives.

4. True or False: Chronically delinquent adolescents often come from families that are low in warmth and high in conflict. (Chapter 16, p. 634)

5. True or False: During emerging adulthood, young people are more susceptible to negative life events due to decreased resilience. (Chapter 17, p. 657)

Segment 47
Transition from College to Adult Life

Khalia and Jasmyne are close friends and university classmates who are now facing a turning point in their lives: the transition from college to adult life. In this segment, the young women discuss their relationships with their families, their future plans, and their hopes and fears as they prepare to leave their college years behind and assume adult roles.

For Discussion

1. Consider Khalia's statement that she "hasn't exactly found" her adult identity. How does this reflect the exploratory nature of emerging adulthood? (Chapter 17, pp. 644–645)

   _____

   _____

   _____

   _____

2. Recall the information about gender and career planning from your text. Do Khalia and Jasmyne have "split dreams"? Why or why not? (Chapter 17, p. 652)

   _____

   _____

   _____

   _____

3. How has attending a large university affected these young women's worldviews? Give specific examples. (Chapter 17, pp. 648–649)

   _____

   _____

   _____

   _____

4. Do Khalia and Jasmyne seem to define themselves in terms of their family roles, or have they begun to establish new, adult identities? Explain.

   _____

   _____

   _____

   _____

Test Your Understanding

1. Constructing a _____ is central to forming an adult identity. (Chapter 17, p. 654)
   A. split dream
   B. vision of spirituality
   C. moral system
   D. worldview

2. Young women's career ambitions often decline during the college years, due to _____. (Chapter 17, p. 652)
   A. lack of assistance from mentors
   B. doubts about their abilities and concerns about balancing work and family life
   C. educational experiences that fail to emphasize the achievements of women
   D. discrimination against ethnic minorities

3. True or False: College students tend to move from relativistic thinking, which views all knowledge as embedded in a framework of thought, toward dualistic thinking, which compares beliefs to objective standards. (Chapter 17, p. 648)

4. Feelings of _____ peak in the late teens and early twenties, as young people move through a series of school and employment settings. (Chapter 17, p. 656)
   A. loneliness
   B. inadequacy
   C. stranger anxiety
   D. self-efficacy

5. True or False: Young people from high-SES families are more likely to explore many opportunities during the period of emerging adulthood than their low-SES or ethnic minority peers. (Chapter 17, p. 645)

Answer Key for "Test Your Understanding" Questions

Segment 1: Down Syndrome

1. D
2. C
3. less
4. A
5. True

Segment 2: Parenting a Child with a Genetic Disorder

1. D
2. False
3. A
4. False
5. B

Segment 3: Rearing Multiples: Twins and Triplets

1. A
2. True
3. False
4. C
5. D

Segment 4: Reproductive Technology

1. B
2. C
3. C
4. D
5. A

Segment 5: International Adoption

1. True
2. D
3. C
4. True
5. bicultural

Segment 6: Childbirth

1. transition
2. B
3. A
4. False
5. True

Segment 7: Preterm Birth

1. True
2. A
3. D
4. False
5. C

Segment 8: Transition to Parenthood

1. False
2. B
3. A
4. D
5. False

Segment 9: Newborn Reflexes

1. B
2. A
3. C
4. False
5. B

Segment 10: Motor Development in Infancy

1. True
2. A
3. C
4. gross; fine
5. False

Segment 11: Language Development and Literacy

1. D
2. joint
3. True
4. False
5. B

Segment 12: Early Emotional Development

1. basic; self-conscious
2. A
3. False
4. B
5. True

Segment 13: Custodial Grandparents

1. B
2. True
3. True
4. A
5. D

Segment 14: Early Morally Relevant Self-Control

1. False
2. Girls
3. False
4. B
5. A

Segment 15: Piaget's Cognitive-Developmental Theory

1. True
2. D
3. C
4. are
5. B

Segment 16: Piagetian Tasks

1. B
2. refutes
3. D
4. A
5. False

Segment 17: Children's Understanding of Death

1. True
2. refutes
3. False
4. D
5. True

Segment 18: Vygotsky's Sociocultural Theory

1. Piaget; Vygotsky
2. D
3. zone of proximal development
4. B
5. True

Segment 19: Memory: Recognition, Recall, and Memory Strategies

1. B
2. Recognition; Recall
3. False
4. C
5. True

Segment 20: Autobiographical Memory

1. script
2. securely
3. B
4. D
5. True

Segment 21: Understanding of False Belief

1. B
2. True
3. B
4. False
5. A

Segment 22: Autism

1. A
2. B
3. False
4. True
5. D

Segment 23: Quality Child Care

1. True
2. D
3. exceeds
4. B
5. D

Segment 24: Jumpstart: Promoting Early Literacy and School Readiness

1. False
2. C
3. D
4. A
5. True

Segment 25: Playful Learning in Early Childhood

1. True
2. A
3. B
4. False
5. A

Segment 26: Moral Reasoning and Distributive Justice

1. externally; internal
2. True
3. B
4. C
5. Social conventions

Segment 27: Child Abuse

1. A
2. B
3. False
4. A
5. D

Segment 28: Childhood Obesity

1. A
2. D
3. False
4. C
5. False

Segment 29: ADHD

1. B
2. A
3. C
4. D
5. True

Segment 30: Cooperative Learning

1. D
2. True
3. B
4. Multigrade
5. False

Segment 31: First-Grade Science Education

1. cooperative learning
2. False
3. D
4. True
5. B

Segment 32: Dramatic Arts Education

1. D
2. A
3. True
4. False
5. C

Segment 33: Revitalizing an Inner-City School

1. B
2. True
3. C
4. True
5. A

Segment 34: School-Community Partnership: After-School Enrichment Activities

1. A
2. C
3. False
4. True
5. A

Segment 35: Self-Concept in Childhood and Adolescence

1. False
2. D
3. B
4. C
5. True

Segment 36: Peer Harassment

1. cyberbullying
2. True
3. C
4. True
5. B

Segment 37: Divorce and Father Custody

1. C
2. more
3. C
4. False
5. A

Segment 38: Homosexuality

1. B
2. D
3. earlier
4. False
5. True

Segment 39: Adolescent Parenthood

1. False
2. False
3. C
4. B
5. D

Segment 40: Adolescent Friendship

1. True
2. increases
3. A
4. B
5. False

Segment 41: Adolescent Dating

1. C
2. A
3. D
4. D
5. False

Segment 42: Civic Engagement in Adolescence

1. C
2. B
3. True
4. D
5. True

Segment 43: Changing Parent-Adolescent Relationships

1. B
2. B
3. True
4. False
5. A

Segment 44: Delinquency

1. B
2. supports
3. C
4. B
5. True

Segment 45: Identity and Emerging Adulthood

1. dualistic; relativistic
2. A
3. True
4. C
5. D

Segment 46: Resilience: From Gang Member to Responsible Adult

1. C
2. D
3. A
4. True
5. False

Segment 47: Transition from College to Adult Life

1. D
2. B
3. False
4. A
5. True